EASTERN CHRISTIAN LITURGIES

The Armenian, Coptic, Ethiopian and Syrian Rites

EASTERN CHRISTIAN LITURGIES

The Armenian, Coptic, Ethiopian and Syrian Rites

Eucharistic Rites with
Introductory Notes and Rubrical Instructions

Peter D. Day

IRISH UNIVERSITY PRESS
Shannon · Ireland

ISBN 0 7165 0595 9

Microfilm, microfiche and other forms of micro-publishing
© Irish University Microforms Shannon Ireland

Irish University Press Shannon Ireland
T. M. MacGlinchey   Publisher

FILMSET, PRINTED AND BOUND IN THE REPUBLIC OF IRELAND
AT SHANNON BY ROBERT HOGG, PRINTER TO
IRISH UNIVERSITY PRESS.

Dedication

To my wife and family, who endured the writing of this book and for whose encouragement and assistance I shall be always grateful.

Contents

Illustrations

Acknowledgments

I wish to acknowledge the assistance and co-operation of the following who have helped to make the production of this book easier: Miss Baird, B.A., F.L.A., and Miss Greenhill, of the Brighton Public Reference Library; Miss Eileen Hollingdale, A.L.A., of Rottingdean Public Library; Mrs Frances Folley of Saltdean; the Rt. Rev. Brion de Fouesnel of Sydney, Australia; Mesrob Vardapet Ashjian of the Armenian Theological Seminary, Antelias, Lebanon; the Rt. Rev. Alexander Turner of the Syrian Orthodox Archdiocese, Mount Vernon, New York; the Trustees of the Irish Central Library for Students; the Cork County Library; the British Museum; the Rev. Paul Verghese of the Orthodox Theological Seminary, Kottayam, Kerala, India; the Rev. Carl Q. Lee of the Christian Catholic Church, Zion, Illinois; the Rev. M. A. Joseph of the Syrian Orthodox Church, Singapore; the Rev. Mathew Kadakampallil of Trivandrum, India; the Rt. Rev. A. Paulos Txadua of Addis Ababa, Ethiopia; the Rt. Rev. Youhanna Nouer of Assiut, United Arab Republic.

General Introduction

The liturgical rites of Christendom can be reduced to four general categories: the Antiochene, Alexandrian, Roman and Gallican. From one or other of these four different rite 'types' all extant liturgies are derived, usually not directly but through a process of development involving combinations and borrowings.

The diagram which appears below traces the development of the various liturgical forms that we have today in relation to their respective origins.

It is from the Antiochene and Alexandrian rites that all Eastern rites have sprung, while the Roman rite, though having undergone many changes, has had no offspring, though it has fathered many local 'usages'. The Gallican rites can be said to constitute a family of liturgies standing midway between the Eastern and Western forms.

In the Eastern Christian churches of today there are basically five distinct rites that enjoy wide usage, namely the Antiochene, Byzantine, Armenian, East Syrian and Alexandrian.

The present volume treats of the Syrian, Armenian, Coptic and Ethiopian liturgies. Some conservatives might consider the translations a little too familiar; the writer hopes that this is their only complaint.

In subsequent volumes the Byzantine, Maronite, Chaldean, Syro-Malabar, Nestorian and Syro-Malankar rites will be dealt with, as also the liturgy of the Western Orthodox Church in France, the U.K. and the U.S.A. A compendium of little-used but important Anaphoras of the Eastern churches will be included in volume 3.

Basically there are two major historical events that must be borne in mind when studying the rather complex matrix of Eastern Christian liturgical forms. These are the Nestorian Schism that followed the Council of Ephesus in 431 and the Monophysite Schism which was a consequence of the Council of Chalcedon in 451.

From these two schisms many dissident churches emerged and it is my intention throughout these volumes briefly to outline the varying practices of the dissident churches by way of contrast with the standard Eastern Catholic practice, which, of course, will be outlined also.

The dissident churches of the East are: (1) the Nestorian family of churches which exists throughout Iraq and Syria, (2) the Monophysite churches which include the Syrian Jacobite Church, the Coptic Church of Egypt, the Ethiopian Church, the Armenian Church and the Malabar-Jacobite Church in India, and (3) the Orthodox family of churches, which are made up of the ancient Patriarchates of Constantinople, Alexandria, Antioch and Jerusalem, together with many other independent churches.

The Catholic churches of the East include those of the (1) Byzantine Rite, (2) the Alexandrian Rite, including the Coptic and Ethiopic Uniate churches, (3) the Antiochene Rite, including the Syrians, Maronites and Malankarese churches, (4) the Armenian Rite and (5) the Chaldean Rite which includes the Malabarese.

The principal liturgical difference between the East and the West is to be found in the fact that Eastern Orthodoxy developed in a predominately Greek cultural environment, while the Roman system developed out of a Latin mentality.

Latin, with its predilection for precision and definition, lends itself ideally to formulation and codification while the Greek ethos allows subtleties and finer shades of meaning, This conclusion is quite apparent when the Eastern and Western styles of theology are compared.

There is, however, a basic unity prevailing between the East and the West, in that both accept the same scriptural tradition, both affirm belief in Jesus Christ, God Incarnate, both accept the Holy Trinity and the necessity of the sacraments, especially those of baptism and the Eucharist, and both affirm a belief in the survival of man after death.

Eastern Christian worship differs in many ways from that of the West in the liturgical forms employed and the roles played by the clergy and laity alike. The difference is also evidenced in the architectural design of their churches and the decorations employed.

Eastern Orthodox churches are generally small and may be either cruciform, after a Greek style of cross, or quite small and round, rather like the Ethiopian churches. In the following volumes the reader will become aware of the immense variety of interior designs prevailing throughout the Christian East. Most Eastern churches have the distinctive iconostasis, basically a screen, often heavily decorated, in which are set three doors separating the sanctuary or east end, from the west end of the church.

In spite of the great variety of liturgical rites throughout the Christian East used in the celebration of the Eucharist, there is general conformity to a basic pattern: the central part of the liturgy, the Anaphora, is similar throughout the East. It commences with the Preface, which is of invariable form, preceding the Sanctus and Words of Institution and followed by the Epiclesis or invocation of the Holy Spirit upon the Oblation. The Anaphora is usually brought to a close with the Great Intercession, the Fraction and then the Communion.

From the liturgies which follow it will be seen that the position of
the Great Intercession is far from invariable; for example, it precedes
the Epiclesis among the Chaldeans but follows it among users of the
Byzantine Rite.

Eastern Christians prefer to call the sacraments 'Mysteries' (*mysterion*;
Slavonic *tainstvo*). The preference for this term highlights the peculiar
mysticism which pervades the whole of Eastern theology, as against
the more legalistic and definitive approach of Western theology.

In the early days of Christianity there was never felt to be any need
to define or explain the workings of the sacraments and this was left to
the Scholastics of the thirteenth century, who felt that the form,
purpose and matter of each sacrament was in need of clarification.
Their excessive ecclesiastical legalism was not indulged in by Eastern
scholars, who, while accepting the seven sacraments approved by
Rome, still considered the blessing of the waters at Epiphany and the
taking of vows by a monk or nun to be sacraments.

In the East a person is baptized by triple immersion and the formula
used—'The servant of God, N., is baptized . . .'—serves to stress the
corporateness of the initiation by which the Church receives a new
member. In the West, by contrast, the formula 'I baptize . . .' emphasizes
the initiation of the new member by virtue of an individual sacerdotal
authority.

With regards chrismation or confirmation, in the East this sacrament
is administered immediately upon baptism. Among Eastern Christians
the holy chrism is consecrated by the head of each national church in
the presence of a gathering of bishops, which serves to emphasize the
blessing of a united episcopate. This sacrament has been called a
sacrament of Christian unity, because, just as all members are anointed
with the same chrism, so they are brought into the communion of the
same body.

There is a similarity between the form used by the priest in administering this sacrament and that used by the Jews at circumcision (cf.
Gen 17:11; Rom 4:11). The priest's words are: 'The Seal of the Holy
Spirit . . .'. Discounting obvious differences, I do not accept the view
that the similarity is simply accidental.

Penance in the East is administered in quite a different way from
that of the West. In the East the penitent stands in front of a lectern
upon which the book of Gospels and a hand cross are placed, and the
priest stands beside him. There is very little formalism in this sacrament
and the method employed by the confessor varies from priest to priest.
The confession concludes with the prayer of absolution.

In the Russian Church, the formula shows evidence of a borrowing
from the West; it is quite unlike any other Orthodox or Eastern church

formula, by reason of its use of the pronoun 'I'. 'May our Lord and God, Jesus Christ, through the grace and bounty of his love towards mankind, forgive you, N., all your sins, and I, an unworthy priest, through the power given to me by him, do forgive and absolve you from all your sins.'

In the East, the frequency and practice vary from rite to rite, in fact in some churches only specially selected priests may hear confession.

As to the administration of holy unction, the Eastern churches differ significantly from the West, in that they prefer to have several priests administer the sacrament together, the ideal number being seven. This preference again serves to emphasize the fact that the healing power of the Church properly belongs to the Church as a whole and not to the individual priest.

In the bestowal of orders, the practice in the East is again quite different from that of the West, in that the bishop lays his hand on the ordinand's head, after the congregation has actively expressed its approval. There have been many occasions on which this approval has not been forthcoming; the laity's approval is far from a purely formal aquiescence.

The sacrament of marriage throughout the East is poetically referred to as the 'crowning'. This crowning takes place in representation of the symbolic union between Christ and his Church. The priest then blesses the couple with the words: 'O Lord our God, crown them with glory and honour.' The crowns are retained until the close of the ceremony. An epistle and gospel are read, and following the Lord's Prayer, the couple drink wine from the same cup; then they are lead three times around the lectern, while the choir sings appropriate hymns.

While the Orthodox allow remarriage after divorce, on certain grounds, or death of the other party, the second ceremony is quite restrained and almost penitential in nature.

A.   The Antiochene liturgical family

There are two basic rites of this family, the West Syrian and the Maronite.

1) The West Syrian rite is used in the Syriac and Arabic languages by the Jacobites and West Syrian Catholics of Syria, Iraq and Lebanon. The Syriac used by the Arabic-speaking Jacobites is a Syriac with Western pronunciation and characters. The Jacobite liturgy is named after St James the Apostle. The Anaphora has about seventy alternatives, but among them the one most commonly used is that attributed to St Eustathius, which is characterized by its brevity.

In India this rite is celebrated in Malayalam, a language related to Tamil, and used by the Jacobites and the Malankarese Catholics.

Among the Jacobites in India it seems that the inaudible prayers are occasionally recited in Syriac.

2) The Maronite rite is a variation of the West Syrian rite and will be treated in full in volume 2. At its very best it could be considered highly latinized in form and is employed by the Maronite Catholics of Syria and Lebanon. It is celebrated in both the Syriac and Arabic languages. The rubrics are published in the Karshuni dialect.

B.   The Byzantine liturgical family

In this family one sees the undoubted influence of Antioch and Jerusalem. This rite, to be fully dealt with in volume 2, is used in all Orthodox churches, and by the Catholic Melkites, Ruthenians, Russians and Rumanians, and many other language-groups. The languages used include Greek, Rumanian, Staroslav and Arabic.

The Byzantine Church has three principal liturgies, that of St John Chrysostom, that of St Basil the Great and that of the Pre-Sanctified (or the Liturgy of St Gregory of Rome). There is a fourth liturgy, that of St James the Apostle, but it is rarely celebrated.

C.   The Armenian liturgical family

This liturgical family developed out of a combination of Syrian and Cappadocian influences, within a matrix derived from Jerusalem with subsequent Byzantine and Latin accretions.

The Armenian Church is unique in having only one rite, which appears to combine the liturgies of St John Chrysostom and that of St James. The composite liturgy is given the name of St Gregory the Illuminator.

The Armenian rite (volume 1) is used by dissident and Catholic alike, with very little difference.

D.   The East Syrian liturgical family

This liturgical family developed at Edessa, though the people of Mesopotamia were evangelized from Antioch. The East Syrian rite (volume 3) is used in Syria and Iraq by the Nestorians, as also by the Catholic Chaldeans of Iraq.

The East Syrian liturgical family makes use of three liturgies. The one most frequently used is that known as the Liturgy of the Apostles which allegedly goes back to the very foundation of the Persian Christian community. There is also the Liturgy of St Theodore which is sung on Sundays from Advent until Palm Sunday and the Liturgy of Nestorius which is celebrated only five times a year—on the feasts of the Epiphany and of St John the Baptist, on Maundy Thursday and on Wednesday and Thursday during the Feast of Nineveh (a period of three days a fortnight before Lent), which is reputed to commemorate the incident recorded in the Book of Jonah 3:5,10.

The Nestorians use Syriac as their liturgical language, but with less vernacular than that used by the West Syrian rite. The Catholic Chaldeans use pure Syriac, with Eastern pronunciations and characters, but the scriptural lessons are read out in the vernacular.

E.   The Alexandrian liturgical family

The original Greek liturgy of Alexandria was translated into Coptic and underwent very strong Syrian influence. It subsequently bifurcated into the Coptic and Ethiopian rites, which are fully dealt with in the present volume.

Among the Catholic Copts the liturgical language is Coptic with the addition of many Greek words, but frequently Arabic is used in the liturgy in preference to Coptic. The Monophysite Copts use much the same language pattern as the Catholics.

The Copts of Egypt have three principal liturgies, the most ancient being that of St Clement which is celebrated on Friday in Passion Week, the other two liturgies being those of St Gregory and St Basil. The former is used on Christmas Day, the Epiphany and Easter Sunday, while the Liturgy of St Basil is used generally throughout the year.

The liturgical language in use among the Ethiopians is Ge'ez, which is the ancient and literary Ethiopic tongue, rather similar to Arabic, but which has been defunct since the thirteenth century. The seventeen different Ethiopian liturgies are all derived from the Coptic rite.

OUR LORD'S WORDS OF INSTITUTION

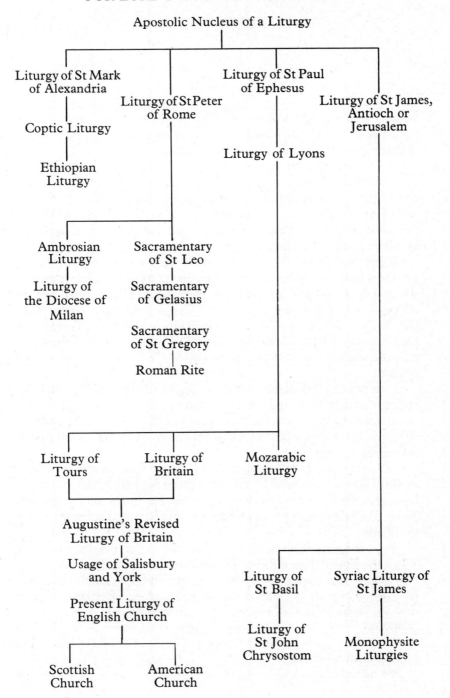

Apostolic Nucleus of a Liturgy

Liturgy of St Mark of Alexandria

Liturgy of St Peter of Rome

Liturgy of St Paul of Ephesus

Liturgy of St James, Antioch or Jerusalem

Coptic Liturgy

Liturgy of Lyons

Ethiopian Liturgy

Ambrosian Liturgy

Sacramentary of St Leo

Liturgy of the Diocese of Milan

Sacramentary of Gelasius

Sacramentary of St Gregory

Roman Rite

Liturgy of Tours

Liturgy of Britain

Mozarabic Liturgy

Augustine's Revised Liturgy of Britain

Usage of Salisbury and York

Present Liturgy of English Church

Liturgy of St Basil

Syriac Liturgy of St James

Liturgy of St John Chrysostom

Monophysite Liturgies

Scottish Church

American Church

The Armenian Liturgy

INTRODUCTION

1. *History*

According to legendary accounts, Christianity was originally brought to Armenia by St Bartholomew and St Thaddaeus. This is quite dubious and possibly belongs to the realm of myth.

The 'revival' of Christianity is attributed to the efforts of St Gregory the Illuminator (Srbotz Grigor Lusavoritsh), whose dead hand is still used for the blessing of the new patriarch. Gregory the Illuminator was born between the years 233 and 255. After the death of his parents, he was brought up by a Christian nurse. He married and had two sons, who became bishops of Armenia.

Gregory found a place at court, but on account of his refusal to offer sacrifices to idols and his zeal for Christianity he was thrown into a pit where he languished for fourteen years; during this time he was allegedly fed by a widow called Anna. Gregory was able to cure King Tiridate's illness miraculously, for which he was released. Subsequently the king was converted and baptized. This conversion had the effect that the whole country officially embraced Christianity as the official religion.

Gregory travelled widely and according to Eusebius (*H.E.*, IX, 8) he speedily consolidated the country's conversion. In 302 Gregory was consecrated by Leontius, the metropolitan of Caesarea in Cappadocia. After the break with Caesarea, the primates in Armenia took the title of catholicos and patriarch.

St Gregory retired to a monastery on Mount Manyea, where he died in 331. He was succeeded by his son, Aristaces or Rhestakes, who was present at the Council of Nicaea in 325; his eldest brother, Vertannes, succeeded Aristaces in 339, and Vertannes was in turn succeeded by his son Yusik.

The country was constantly under invasion or the threat of conquest. When the Zoroastrian Persians invaded Armenia with the intention of completely subjugating them they also attempted to impose Zoroastrianism upon them. This led to revolt and the Persian monarch relented in his efforts to subjugate the Armenians and granted them religious liberty. It has been suggested that these internal troubles and unrest were responsible for the aloofness of the Armenians during the Monophysite troubles.

The national synod of the Armenian Church repudiated the Council of Chalcedon (451), and this rejection was confirmed by the two councils of Tuin (524? and 552). The rejection of the Council has also been attributed to the careless and incompetent transcriptions of its decrees from the Greek language into Armenian. The rejection was also complicated by the fact that ten representatives of the Armenian Church were present at the Council and that they were signatories of its Acts.

At the beginning of the fifth century the church began to show signs of growth and progress with the development and popularity of cenobitic monasticism. Certainly there had been many hermits before this, but their way of life had been characteristically unorganized.

Under the leadership of Isaac the Great, the church's separation from Byzantium and its emperor—with the autonomy which was a consequence—was given an impetus by the work of a monk named Mesrop. He introduced the national alphabet, which allowed the ordinary people to read religious texts without requiring a knowledge of either Syriac or Greek. Mesrop was also partly responsible for translating the Bible from the Syriac Peshitto into Armenian. This text was later improved by collating it with good manuscripts and the Greek New Testament.

The acceptance of Monophysitism and the rejection of Chalcedon was dictated by a desire to promote the country's independence from Byzantium; the Council was viewed as the work of the emperor. In 591 the Greek emperor, having taken most of Armenia from the Persians, summoned a council of Armenian bishops. Not surprisingly, this council gave its approval of the Council of Chalcedon and named an Orthodox catholicos to be head of the Armenian Church; Bishop John, who was so elected, established his residence at Avan. Those clergy who did not live in the part of the country under Byzantine control would not assent to this council's action and decisions, and so a schism came about. It can be concluded that the Armenians held to their Monophysitism as a symbol of their independence of Constantinople.

The coming of the Arabs presented a new threat to the religious liberty and political freedom of the Armenians. The fighting which lasted from the middle of the seventh century until the middle of the ninth century gave the Arabs much the same power over the Armenians as the Persians had exercised.

Nevertheless religious freedom was enjoyed by the Armenians on the whole and despite further attempts by Byzantium to bring about conformity with the Catholic Church, they remained uninterested and replied by a further renouncement of the Council of Chalcedon by means of a national council convened in 719 at Tovin (Duin), under the Patriarch John VI. This synod decreed (1) the use of an unmixed chalice (i.e., only wine in the chalice) and unleavened bread in the celebration of the liturgy; (2) the transfer of the observance of Christmas from 25 December to January, as part of the Epiphany celebrations; (3) abstinence from fish, oil, eggs and butter during Lent, except on Saturdays and Sundays; (4) the suspension of the liturgy on Maundy Thursday. The effect of this synod was to divide the Armenians into those of Greater Armenia, who accepted these resolutions, and those of Lesser Armenia, who were and continued to remain under Byzantine influence.

In 924, civil wars and the unrest which followed caused the Armenian patriarch to move to Aghtmar, an island in Lake Van. The continuous struggles with foreign powers persisted for four centuries. In the early part of the ninth century until about 1080, the country was under the power of the Caliph of Baghdad, but about 1050, with the advent of fresh Turkish invasions, the country became split up into principalities under rulers who were either Turks or Kurds. A consequence of all this was the gradual weakening of the central ecclesiastical authority and power with the constant change of the patriarchal seat; in 1100 there were four prelates, each claiming to be the representative of St Gregory and each condemning the others as usurpers. By 1102 a dispute arose between the Greeks and the Armenians which has remained unresolved ever since—the disagreement on the dating of the Easter observance.

The coming of the Crusaders from the West, together with the establishment of the Armenian kingdom in Cilicia, to the west of Armenia proper, brought the church into closer contact with the Greeks and the Catholics of Western Europe. Attempts at negotiations with the Byzantine Church failed, because of the stronger Latin influence. The rulers of Cilician Armenia sought assistance from the Crusaders, which resulted in the establishment of very strong relations between the Armenian and Catholic churches. Many Armenians submitted to the Catholic Church. In fact when King Leo II was crowned, the Catholicos Gregory VI proclaimed the union of the Armenian Church with Rome; of course this only applied to southern Armenia. In 1307 a council was held by the latinized Armenians, in which the error of Monophysitism was formally rejected and condemned. However, when Lesser Armenia fell in 1375, the bonds between Armenia and Rome broke. In succeeding years, it is very difficult to say which of the patriarchs remained united with the West.

The Council of Florence in 1439 represented yet another attempt at unification by the Armenians. At that Council a liturgically disastrous attempt was made to try to impose Western usages upon the Armenians. The dissidents looked to the Turks for assistance in resisting and denouncing these attempts, particularly in view of France's political interest in the consequence of a drift towards Rome.

Plans for reunion were given a fresh setback when Armenia was

divided into two jurisdictions, that of Sis in Cilicia, and that of Etchmi-
adzin in Greater Armenia, each with its own catholicos. The catholicos
in Greater Armenia was generally regarded as being devoted to the
cause of unity with Rome. This sector of the Armenian Church was
considerably latinized, which influence is still visible. Some of the
catholicoi of Sis were quite friendly to Rome, though some remained
openly hostile.

In 1742 Pope Benedict XIV (1740–58), who was most concerned with
the state of Eastern Christianity, established a patriarchal See at Kraim,
the administrative centre of which was later moved to Bzommar, near
Beirut.

By 1830, thanks to French pressure, the Turks recognized the
Catholic Armenians as a separate millet or nation, with the archbishop
as its civil head. With the election of Archbishop Antony Hassun as
patriarch, many jurisdictional questions were settled, particularly that
concerning the primacies of Constantinople and Cilicia.

Protestant missionary activity became very much in evidence at this
time. Many colleges and seminaries were opened and the Bible was
translated into the vernacular. Although it has been suggested that the
missionaries were not intending to convert the Armenians, nevertheless
many conservatives became alarmed and brought influence to bear
upon the Armenian patriarch in Constantinople to formally excommunicate those who followed the missionaries.

A synod held in Rome in 1911 regulated many liturgical matters of
concern to the Armenians; but the revisions were Western. The
language of the liturgy, as it is today, was to be classical Armenian,
though the Gospel could be read unceremoniously a second time in
modern Armenian or any other language.

From the time of the massacres of 1890 onwards until 1915 and the
exodus which followed in 1921, consequent upon the establishment
of a Soviet Socialist Republic in Russian Armenia, the plight of the
Armenians, Catholic and non-Catholic alike, who found themselves
separated from their fellows, has been most distressing indeed.

The full title of the Catholic Armenian patriarch is 'the Patriarch
of the Catholic Armenians and Catholicos of Cilicia.' All the patriarchs
take the name of Peter upon election. The full title of the Monophysite
patriarch is 'the Servant of God, the Supreme Patriarch and Catholicos
of the Armenians'. The Monophysite patriarch is elected by a national
church assembly, which is made up of bishops and lay delegates. It is
the patriarch who consecrates bishops and the chrism for distribution
throughout the world.

II.   Church Buildings

Armenian churches are built so that the altar faces the East. The interior is divided into four parts: the sanctuary or *srbaran*, within which are the altar or *surb* and sacristy or *avandatoun*; the choir or *bem*; the nave; and the porch. An interesting feature of Armenian churches is the absence of an iconostasis, which would conceal the altar from view; in fact the altar is always visible, except during a few solemn parts of the liturgy, when it is concealed by the use of curtains or *waraguir*. The smaller curtain is drawn during the celebrant's communion, while the larger curtain is opened and closed more frequently, but is kept drawn throughout Lent.

The altar or throne is made of stone, but unlike the Western altar it tends to be oblong and recesses into the screen which extends across the apse against the east wall of the sanctuary. The altar is not flush with the east wall, but permits the passage of clergy behind it. To a Westerner, the altar appears a little bizarre, on account of the large number of decorations and ornaments, which reduce the mensa of the altar to a mere shelf. The altar usually has several gradines, above which stands a cross, set into an alcove centrally placed at the top.

The area of the sanctuary is raised some distance above the choir by up to half a dozen steps and often there may be two small staircases leading from the sanctuary to the choir below. In front of the altar is a low communion rail, then the choir, and then another lower communion rail, behind which the men are accommodated, and behind them, the women.

Only priests and clerics may enter the sanctuary. When they do so, they must put on slippers or sandals, which are kept exclusively for the service of the church. In the sanctuary, on either side of the altar, there are two doors leading to the vestry and sacristy respectively. Before these doors, credence tables are placed; the table on the north side, against the vestry door, serves as prothesis table or *matouthsaran*.

In the *bem* or choir there are no stalls as such. When the lessons are to be read a folding lectern may be brought out, covered with a cloth and stood in the middle. There is no fixed pulpit, but when a sermon is to be given, a movable pulpit may be erected at the door of the choir; the patriarch alone has the privilege of preaching from the sanctuary.

The choir is usually made up of boys. Together with the choir leader, they stand in a semi-circle and accompany the celebrant with appropriate chants. Music is provided by cymbals and bells as well as an instrument called a *quecone*, which is a staff surmounted by a cherub's figure; bells are attached to the staff. Occasionally the deacon may manipulate this instrument during the solemn parts of the liturgy.

There is no seating accommodation allowed except for the bishop, who has a seat placed on the left side of the altar. The rest of the clergy are expected either to stand throughout the liturgy or sit cross-legged on mats or carpets on the floor, according to the local custom.

St Vartan Armenian Cathedral, New York (Altar not installed)

One curious feature often encountered in Armenian churches is the ostrich eggs suspended from the ceiling. They serve as a symbol of the resurrection. One possible explanation, current among the Copts, is that the eggs are symbols of faith, since the ostrich is reputed to hatch her eggs by hopefully gazing at them.

The remainder of the church's interior is divided into two sections, one for men and one for women; the women are usually separated from the men by a screen or gallery. In those churches which are heavily influenced by the West, seating accommodation is provided; otherwise the floor is covered with mats. On entering a church, the shoes are removed and one sits cross-legged on the floor. Often spitoons are provided.

Upon the altar one finds a book of the Gospels and a copy of the Divine Liturgy, which is kept on the Epistle or south side of the altar. The Blessed Sacrament is reserved and its presence is indicated by a sanctuary light.

Most Armenian churches are dedicated to the Holy Trinity, the Blessed Saviour, the Holy Cross, the Blessed Virgin, St Gregory the Illuminator and other early Christian saints.

III.   *Altar vessels*

The chalice and paten are usually of Western size and dimension, and during the preparatory rites of the liturgy they are kept covered with a veil.

The bread or *neshkhar* in use is unleavened. It is prepared by a priest early in the morning; if a bishop is to celebrate, it is prepared by one of his deacons. The bread differs from the Western wafer in being a little thicker and less crisp; it has a figure of Christ stamped upon it. The wine used is pure fermented grape juice known as Shiraz wine.

Among the Monophysites, Communion is given to the laity under both species, by intinction. The priest takes the bread in his hand—or in some rare cases, in a spoon—and dips it into the chalice. Catholic Armenians, however, are bound by the usual Roman regulations.

In common with other Eastern rites, the liturgy may be celebrated only once on the same altar during the day, and it may not be offered after noon, except at Christmas, Easter and Holy Thursday. The frequency of celebration varies, but normally among the Monophysite Armenians there is a celebration only on Sundays, Thursdays and Saturdays; during Lent, it is celebrated much more frequently.

IV.   *Language and rite*

The language employed in the liturgy is ancient Armenian and none other. The rite is a modification of the Liturgy of St Basil and in practice there is no tradition of concelebration. In ancient times there were at least ten Anaphoras, as well as the Rite of the Pre-sanctified (*Nakharrbeal*), but there is no trace of these today.

Eight liturgical books are in use by the Armenians:

1) the Directory or Calendar, *Donatsoitz*, which corresponds to the Byzantine Typikon;

2) the Liturgy, which normally contains only what the celebrant and deacon say;

3) the Lectionary, which includes those parts said by the deacon and server;

4) the Book of Ordinations, which is often bound together with the Book of the Liturgy;

5) the Hymn Book, *Dagharan*, containing the hymns sung by the choir during the liturgy;

6) the Book of Hours, *Jamakirkh*, which corresponds to the Divine Office and sometimes includes the Diakonika of the Liturgy;

7) the Book of Canticles, *Sharagan*, which contains the text of the hymns sung in the Office;

8) the Ritual or *Mashdotz*, which contains the texts and rubrics for the administration of the other sacraments.

v. *Vestments*

A cap or crown, called the *saghavart*, is worn. This is usually quite elaborately designed and colourful. The *shapik* approximates to the Western alb, but differs in being fuller and composed usually of silk. The stole or *porurar* differs from the Western stole in that the wearer's head is put through a hole in the upper part of the vestment and the rest hangs down in front. The stole is usually made of very expensive brocade or silk, and is often bejewelled.

The girdle or *goti* secures the stole to the alb and again is often richly embroidered. A large white napkin is attached to the left side of the girdle; it is used to cleanse the fingers or sacred vessels in the event of any defilement.

The maniples or *bazpan* are two slips of brocade attached to the wrists. Originally they were used as towels.

The *varkas* is a vestment peculiar to the Armenians and resembles a small amice with a stiffened collar attached to it, which allows it to stand up around the neck, so as to appear above the *schoorchar* or cope. The *schoorchar* corresponds to the Western chasuble as the principal Eucharistic vestment, but unlike Western copes it lacks a hood. From the varkas a breast-plate embossed with jewels may be suspended; this is said to derive from the Jewish ephod.

It is customary for vartapets (see § viii, below) and honoured priests to wear a pectoral cross; vartapets may also wear the mitre; if a vartapet is an aratshnord—that is, a vartapet exercising episcopal jurisdictiction, rather like a vicar apostolic, without being in episcopal orders—he may use a Latin mitre and crosier.

The crosier carried by bishops is of the Western shape and occasionally the bishop may also wear two strips of brocade, which are attached to the shoulders of the schoorchar. Upon these strips of material one often finds beautiful examples of embroidery displaying pictures of saints.

The dress for a metropolitan is quite different from that of other bishops, in that he may wear a gold mitre and a triple pallium, and use a longer staff, as well as the archiepiscopal *epigonation*, which is basically a lozenge-shaped piece of stiffened material, suspended from the left-hand side of the girdle; it is also called a *konker*. The epigonation is also worn by the catholicos.

During the consecration of the catholicos, his head is covered with a great veil or *kogh*, which is decorated with a golden fringe. It is always carried before him on great feast-days. It covers not only his head, but his shoulders as well. Another distinctive feature of the dress of the catholicos is the pallium which is folded five times across his chest.

The staff used by vartapets, bishops and the catholicos is surmounted by a cross entwined by two serpents.

Deacons may wear the shapik of linen or silk, which is worn ungirdled and is characterized by wide sleeves. The deacon's stole is quite long and is worn over the left shoulder, with the posterior end drawn around, so as to come under the right arm and across the chest.

In common with most Eastern-rite churches, the Armenians do not have any sequence of liturgical colours, as in the West.

The outdoor dress of an unmarried priest consists of a black-purple cassock with a broad belt, over which another loose-fitting gown, the *verarku*, is worn. During the recitation of the Office, a dark-coloured cope may be worn, while in Iran a fur-bordered cap, called the *kulpas*, is put on. Married priests wear a distinctive dark blue cassock with a black gown and blue turban. One distinctive feature of Armenian clerical outdoor dress is the black cap or *pakegh*, which is considerably lower than its Slavonic and Byzantine equivalent, the *kamelafka*. The Armenian pakegh comes to a point, whereas the Slavonic-style kamelafka is flat. All Armenian clergy wear the pakegh, but only the celibate clergy wear it with a veil or *veghar*, which hangs down the back.

VI. *Calendar*

The Armenians date their history from their eponymous founder Haik (2492 B.C.). The Julian reckoning is now in use, but the Armenians do not celebrate Christmas as a separate feast; it is commemorated in conjunction with Epiphany (Hsinuthium). The celebration of Christmas on 25 December is ignored because the Armenians consider this custom to be a Western innovation which was not introduced to the East until the fourth century. Armenia was the one country where it was not introduced, and hence the Armenians are naturally proud of this unique distinction.

In the Armenian calendar there are five classes of festivals:

1) feasts that always occur on Sundays, e.g. Pentecost;

2) Easter and its dependent feasts;

3) immovable feasts, e.g. Nativity, Epiphany and the Baptism of our Blessed Lord, and the Annunciation of the Blessed Virgin Mary.

4) Transferred feasts, e.g. the Transfiguration of our Lord Jesus Christ, the Assumption of the Blessed Virgin Mary, the Feast of all the Holy Apostles. All these feasts are transferred to the following Sunday.

5) Those holy days which occur on a Sunday, Wednesday or Friday and are therefore not observed; some are however transferred to the following Saturday.

Fasting among the Armenians is rigorously observed. Strictly speaking, a fast implies only one meal a day, and that meal should exclude fish, meat, butter and milk. Typical fast days are: the days in Lent with the exception of Sunday, which according to Tournefort is a day on which fish can be eaten with impunity; the long fast of Nineveh, which is also known as 'that of the Fore-runner' (Armenian writers are divided as to its origin: some consider it to be a commemoration of the fast of the Ninevites, while others consider it to be a remembrance of the expulsion of our first parents from paradise); every day in Pentecost week. Though all the fasts are strictly observed, the penitential nature of some ordinary fast days is not reflected in the services of the church.

Allied to fasting and abstinence, there is another form of abstention which is most meticulously and curiously observed and that is abstinence from womenfolk; in fact it is considered virtuous for married clergy to abstain from intercourse before the celebration of the Eucharist.

In the East, Saturday is usually observed as a second Sunday. The Armenians regard Saturday as a day in honour of God the Creator, while Sunday is held to be in commemoration of the new creation or Redemption through our Lord Jesus Christ.

VII. *Holy Scriptures*

As far as the New Testament is concerned, the Gospels, Acts and pauline Epistles were translated into Armenian in the third and fourth centuries, probably from an old Syriac version. According to tradition, the translation was the work of St Mesrop and Sahak. But it is known that after the Council of Ephesus in 431, two Armenians returned from Constantinople with manuscripts from the Lucianic text and proceeded to bring the Armenian text into conformity with the text as it existed elsewhere.

In the Armenian Scriptures, there are a few apocryphal books. In the Old Testament these include the History of Joseph and Asanath and the Testament of the Twelve Patriarchs. The last-mentioned book is thought to have been composed by a Jewish convert at the close of the first century A.D. It was then translated into Armenian, along with the canonical Scriptures. In the New Testament, apocryphal books include the Epistle of the Corinthians to St Paul and the Third Epistle of St Paul to the Corinthians. An apocryphal account of the death of St John is found in all editions of the Armenian Bible; it is considered to have been translated from the Greek into Armenian during the eleventh century.

VIII. *Vartapets*

The office and rank of vartapet is peculiar to the Armenians and is a rank conferred by a kind of ordination rite. The attention given by the Armenians to education is very high and therefore it is not surprising to find that among them there is a distinct order of the hierarchy set aside with this object in mind.

Vartapets are of two classes, minor and major. The staff or *gauazan* which is presented to each vartapet distinguishes the grade: a minor vartapet has a staff surmounted by a cross with only one entwined serpent, while the major vartapet would have two entwined serpents.

All vartapets are celibate priests who follow the Rule of St Basil of Caesarea. Being unmarried, they are not allowed to hear confessions, and thus occupy themselves entirely with preaching and teaching. It is from this body of clergy that the Armenian bishops are chosen. It has already been noted that vartapets have certain privileges with respect to the use of vestments (see § v, above).

The rite of 'ordination' or commissioning of a vartapet involves the handing of the staff by the bishop, following the recitation of several Epistles and Gospels. This ceremony also involves a doctrinal examination, which is conducted liturgically. Then the staff is presented to each candidate ten times, while ten different formulas are repeated, relating to the virtues conferred on each occasion.

IX. *Sacraments*

1) *Baptism*—Among the Armenians this sacrament is conferred with great solemnity. Together with the sacrament of confirmation,

which is usually administered on the same occasion, it makes for quite a lengthy ceremony. It is my intention simply to outline the salient points that emerge from the administration of the sacrament.

On the eighth day after the child's birth the midwife brings the child to the porch of the church, accompanied by the relatives. The child's clothing is loosened, and the priest and other clergy recite psalms. When the child has been blessed upon its forehead and chest, all the assembled people recite the Lord's Prayer. During the recitation of the psalms at the entrance of the church, a single thread of interwoven red and white threads is prepared by the priest. He fastens the thread to a cross, which he lays upon the child about to be baptized.

Many prayers follow, and then the priest takes the child in his arms and turning towards the West says three times: 'We renounce Satan and all his works.' Then turning towards the East, the priest and god-parents affirm their belief in the Christian mysteries of the Trinity, the Incarnation and the Redemption.

A Gospel is then read, Matthew 28:16–20, which relates the com-missioning of the disciples by Christ to baptize in the name of the Trinity. This reading is then followed by the consecration of the font, the water of which is blessed while a prayer similar to the Epiclesis is recited. Following the recitation of more prayers and the recital of the creed, the child is unclothed and the officiant says to the godparents: 'What does the child seek?' The godparent answers: 'Faith, hope, charity and baptism, to be baptized and made righteous.' This is recited three times.

The priest then holds the child, supporting its neck with his left hand. He takes the child's feet in his right hand and dips the child into the font with its feet facing towards the East and the child looking upwards. The child is then made to stand so that its feet touch the bottom of the font, and the priest says: 'N., the servant of God, com-ing by his own will to the state of catechumen and thence to that of baptism, is now baptized by me, in the Name of the Father and of the Son and of the Holy Spirit.' Water is poured over the child at the mention of each sacred name.

Again the child is immersed three times in the water; this last wash-ing is accompanied by a short prayer. Then the priest proceeds to anoint the forehead, eyes, ears, nostrils, mouth, palms, heart, spine and feet. Each anointing is accompanied by a special prayer; for example, for the anointing of the ears: 'N., may this ointment of sanctification make you obedient to the commandments of God.' For the forehead: 'N., may this sweet oil which is poured upon you in the Name of Christ be a seal of the celestial gifts.' This anointing is properly the sacrament of confirmation, whereas the other anointings are purely ceremonial and sacramental acts.

The clothes of the child are then blessed and the plaited red and white thread with the attached cross is placed around the child's neck. The child is then given a candle and in the arms of the priest it is taken to the altar steps, where it is made to bow its head to the Cross. Then the child is returned to the godparent and given Communion.

Often baptism is given after the liturgy of the Eucharist, in which case the priest having dipped his finger into the chalice places it into the baby's mouth, saying 'N., receive the fullness of the Holy Spirit.' Otherwise the priest simply takes the Sacrament out of the tabernacle and makes the sign of the cross with it over the baby's mouth and replaces it in the tabernacle. This is called 'Communion of the lips'.

Another eight days are allowed to transpire, whereupon the priest unfastens the red and white thread. On the fortieth day the child is brought to the door of the church and the priest says a special prayer over both the child and its mother, following which the child is placed on the altar steps and then returned to its mother.

2) *Confirmation or the sacrament of the holy chrism*—The sacrament of chrismation is usually administered as part of the sacrament of baptism by a priest. The holy oil or chrism (*meron*) is consecrated by the catholicos, who blesses it every few years, usually on Maundy Thursday. The oil includes as many as thirty-six aromatics. Some of the old chrism is put into the new, and this is thought to perpetuate the original holy oil which was allegedly blessed by Christ and brought to Armenia by the Apostles.

As noted in §1 above, on baptism, the priest dips his thumb right into the chrism and anoints the child in nine different places. But the actual form of the sacrament consists in signing the forehead with chrism while saying: 'N., may this sweet oil which is poured upon you in the Name of Christ be a seal of the celestial gifts.'

3) *Penance*—Among Catholic Armenians auricular confession has always been the custom, and the sacrament is administered almost the same way as it is in the Latin Church. Monophysite Armenians allow only married priests to hear confessions. The priest sits on the floor of the house or sacristy where the confession is to be heard, while the penitent kneels and relates each sin quite distinctly, avoiding obscure generalities. The Monophysite priest may defer absolution for a few days, whereas the Catholic usually grants absolution immediately, except for a few obvious exceptions.

Armenians are expected to receive this sacrament at least five times a year, and these occasions must include Epiphany and Easter. The practice of receiving absolution as a necessary preliminary to Communion is not universal among the Armenians, but the tendency is there.

4) *The Eucharist*—Among Catholic Armenians, though Communion

under both species may be received, in practice the laity receive only a small particle. Monophysites on the other hand invariably give Communion by intinction, and that to the very young as well.

Armenians are expected to receive this sacrament at least five times a year: Epiphany, Easter, the Dormition of our Lady, the feast of the Transfiguration and the Exaltation of the Holy Cross.

5) *The anointing of the sick*—According to the rubrics, this sacrament properly requires the presence of seven priests, but now in practice this has been modified. Essentially the Armenian rite resembles the rite obtaining among the Copts, who use a seven-branched lamp. The practice of anointing the sick with the oil from a church lamp is quite ancient; St John Chrysostom speaks of it as being most efficacious.

The Catholic Armenians use this sacrament rather as a viaticum, whereas the other Armenians tend to administer it not only to the dying but also to those who are sick, in order to restore their health.

6) *Holy orders*—Dissident and Catholic Armenians alike have four minor and three major orders: doorkeeper, lector, exorcist, acolyte, subdeacon, deacon and priest. All these orders are conferred on Sundays, and the occasion is one of great solemnity.

The rite of psalmist and cleaner is equivalent to the Western rite of tonsure. Strictly speaking, this rite does not confer an order, but serves to separate a man from the lay state and introduce him to the clerical state; as such, this rite serves as the basis of all orders which may be received subsequently. The rite involves the cutting of the candidate's hair by the bishop, who then presents him with a psalter and a broom. Finally the candidate is vested as a cleric.

a) *Doorkeeper*—For this ordination, the candidate is presented with the key of the church and, in company with the deacon, he goes to the door of the church and places the key in the lock, while the choir sings a hymn.

b) *Reader*—The bishop gives the ordinand a book of the Epistles, with the instruction: 'Take this book and be a preacher of God's Word, instructing yourself in it. If you fulfil your duties with a pure mind and heart, then you will have your reward among the saints. Amen.'

c) *Exorcist*—The candidate is presented with a copy of the Ritual, which contains the formula for baptism and exorcisms. The presentation is accompanied by a rather lengthy prayer: 'Take this; treasure in your mind the words written there. I now give authority to place your hands upon the possessed and cause those about to be baptized to renounce the evil one . . . Amen.'

d) *Acolyte*—The bishop presents the ordinand with a candle and candlestick. After a few prayers, the cleric is presented with an empty flagon, while the bishop says: 'Take this flagon, in order to pour wine into the chalice for the Blood of Christ, in the Name of the Father and of the Son and of the Holy Spirit.' The rite concludes with the choir singing a hymn, while the deacon gives another exhortation. The ordination ends with a short prayer and the liturgy of the Eucharist continues.

e) *Subdeacon*—After the eucharistic liturgy has begun, the bishop sits on the throne and the deacon, having presented the candidate to him, reads three lessons, which are usually taken from Isaiah, Hebrews and St Mark. The bishop then places his hands upon the ordinand's head and having presented him with an empty chalice and paten says: 'Take this holy chalice and be authorized to carry it to the holy altar of the Lord, for the great and precious Mystery of Christ our God, to whom belong glory, power and honour, now and forevermore.' Following the recitation of the Lord's Prayer, the liturgy of the Eucharist continues.

f) *Deacon*—This order is conferred in a most solemn manner. After commencing the eucharistic liturgy, the bishop sits on his throne and the candidates are presented to him. Following a liturgical examination, they approach the altar and kneel there. The bishop places his right hand on the head of each candidate and prays, while the choir sings Psalm 119. The bishop again places his hand on the candidate's head and at the conclusion of another prayer the assistant deacon accompanies the ordinand as he turns and faces the congregation. The people signify their approval of the candidate by exclaiming three times: 'He is worthy.' Again the candidate turns towards the bishop. An assistant priest places his hands upon the ordinand's shoulders, and the bishop places his right hand on the ordinand's head, and says: 'The divine and heavenly Gift that ever fulfils the holy needs of the apostolic Church now calls N. from the subdiaconate to the diaconate for the service of the holy Church according to his own and this congregation's testimony.'

The liturgy of the Eucharist then recommences. Following the Creed and the presentation of the gifts, the bishop again sits on the throne and places his right hand on the ordinand's head for the fourth time. He recites a prayer and then vests the deacon in his distinctive stole. The bishop then presents him with the Book of Gospels, after which the deacon rises and incenses the altar three times. Following the bishop's blessing, the new deacon takes his place among the assistant deacons.

g) *Priesthood*—Candidates for the priesthood must be at least in their twenty-sixth year and approved of by the laity. On the night before the ordination it is customary for the bishop to interrogate the candidate and request him to repeat the Confession of Faith. The next day which is usually a Sunday, sees the commencement of the liturgy.

The candidate is presented to the bishop, who blesses him, places his right hand upon his head and vests him in the stole or *ourar*. After the Readings, Epistle and Gospel, the bishop returns to the throne, following the presentation of the gifts upon the altar, and places his right hand upon the candidate's head, reciting two very long prayers which invoke the aid of the Holy Spirit. The priestly robes are then brought to the bishop, who proceeds to bless them and vest the ordinand in them, beginning with the pasbans, then the saghavard or cap, followed by the varkass and then the *schoorchar*; finally the candidate is vested with the girdle. The bishop places his two hands upon the candidate's head and says: 'Take authority from the Holy Spirit to loose and bind men, as our Lord gave authority.'

The ordinand's hands are then anointed with the holy chrism, as in the West, and then the forehead is anointed as well. Finally the bishop presents the ordinand with a chalice and paten holding unconsecrated bread and wine, saying: 'Receive these, because you have received power through the grace of God to consecrate and complete the holy Sacrifice in the name of our Lord Jesus Christ, for the living and the dead.' The new priest is then incensed three times, and having bowed before the altar and the bishop, he proceeds to give the congregation his first blessing.

If an unmarried man is promoted to orders higher than that of acolyte, he is obliged to remain celibate, and as an unmarried man he may become a monk. If a secular priest is widowed, he may not re-marry, nor may he become a bishop.

7) *Matrimony*—Among the Armenians this is a very lengthy rite. It is often referred to as 'the Imposition of the Crown'. On the day of marriage, which is usually a Monday or Thursday, the clergy go to the bride's house, and there the ring and the robes are blessed. With the arrival of the bridegroom, the clergy recite more prayers, and then the wedding party proceeds to the church, accompanied by band music. The relatives carry candles.

Inside the church, the bridal couple stand side by side at the sanctuary gate, and the priest places the Bible on their heads and recites the sacramental form. The choir sings Psalm 21 and the garland for the bridegroom is twined and prepared; and that for the bride is prepared when the choir sings Psalm 45. Following a sermon and more prayers, the celebrant places the crowns upon their heads and then they are both blessed. The nuptial benediction is as follows: 'O Lord, bless this marriage with your eternal blessing; grant that this man and woman may live in the constant practice of faith, hope and charity; endow them with sobriety and inspire them with holy thoughts. Amen.'

During the ceremony the couple receive the Eucharist and finally return to the husband's home. In earlier days, it was common for the couple to continue to wear the garlands for a period of three to eight days and to live apart from each other, but this is not the case today. When widows or widowers remarry, the service is considerably shorter.

x.   *Sources of liturgical texts*

Arakilian, C., *The Armenian Liturgy*, Watertown, Massachusetts, 1951.
Divine Liturgy of the Holy Apostolic Church of Armenia, 1908.
Issaverdenz, F. J., *The Armenian Liturgy*, Venice, 1873.
Liturgie de la Messe Armenienne, Venice, 1851.
Malan, S. C., *Liturgy of the Holy Apostolic Church of Armenia*, 2 volumes,
    London, 1887.
Petit Paroissien des Liturgies Orientales, Libya, 1941.

ARMENIAN LITURGY

Before the vesting of the celebrant, the assistant clergy vest in private and together sing the following antiphonal refrain (Ktzord) and verse (Phokh):

> May your priest be clothed with
> righteousness and may your saints sing
> joyfully.
>   O Lord, remember David and all his
> troubles.

The remainder of Psalm 132 is recited and concludes:

> Glory be to the Father and to the Son and
> to the Holy Spirit. As it was in the beginning,
> is now and shall be forevermore.

Deacon : Again let us peacefully implore the Lord, so that in the unity of faith we may obtain the grace of his mercy. May the almighty God, our Lord, save us and have mercy upon us. Lord have mercy. *(This is repeated twelve times.)*

During the commencement of the hymn 'O eternal, unfathomable Mystery', the priest says the following prayer:

> O our Lord Jesus Christ, who clothed in light came to earth in a most humble way and became man, you were made the eternal High Priest after the Order of Melchisedeck and beautified your holy Church. O almighty Lord who have permitted me to put on the same heavenly robe, consider me, your worthless servant, to be worthy to boldly offer worship to your honour and glory, and to have all the stains of my sins erased and so be bathed in your light. Take away all sin from me, so that I may be considered worthy of your favours. Allow me to enter with priestly glory, so that I may worthily perform your service. In the company of all those who faithfully fulfil your commandments, and like the wise virgins, may I also be prepared for the heavenly marriage feast, so that I may praise you, O Christ, who took away the sins of the world, because you are the holiness of our souls. Glory, dominion and honour are due to you, O beneficent God.

The choir sings the following hymn, which is attributed to Vartapet Khatchandour (1205):

> O eternal, unfathomable Mystery, who beautifully clothed

the heavens and made the abode of God unapproachable to the demons of hell, you created Adam in a most remarkable way, and made him lord over all your creatures, and in the Garden of Eden you dressed him in glorious splendour. Through the sufferings of your only Son, all creation has been renewed and man has regained his lost heritage, which cannot be taken away from him now.

While the next section of the hymn is being sung, the priest takes the saghavart in his hands. The clergy approach the priest and say:

Let us peacefully beg the Lord to mercifully save us. Blessing and glory are due to the Father, the Son, and the Holy Spirit, now and forevermore. Amen.

Meanwhile the choir continues:

May we receive the anointing by the same tongues of fire that descended upon the Apostles in the upper room, together with the blessing of the vestment in which you are so majestically clothed. Just as you are clothed in the glory of holiness, so may we be clothed in truth.

The saghavart is now placed on the priest's head. He prays:

Lord, crown me with the helmet of salvation, so that I may fight against the power of the enemy. I request this favour by the grace of our Lord Jesus Christ, to whom glory, power and honour are due, now and forevermore.

The schapik and porurar are now put on, while the choir continues:

O God, you who created the stars, strengthen our pleadings as we raise up our hands to you.

Priest :   May I be dressed in the joyful robe of salvation and bound with the virtues of salvation, through the grace of our Lord Jesus Christ, to whom glory, power and honour are due, now and forevermore.

The choir continues to sing while the porurar or stole is being put on and the priest says:

May I receive the yoke of righteousness, O Lord, and may my heart be purged of all sinful stains, by the grace of our Lord Jesus Christ, to whom glory, power and honour are due, now and forevermore.

The following section of the hymn is sung by the choir as the priest puts on the goti or girdle, bazpans or maniples, and the varkas or embroidered amice:

Restrain our thoughts, just as a crown covers the hair of the head; may our senses be controlled by the symbol of the crossed stole, which has been decorated in gold and embellished with flowers, like Aaron's mantle, in preparation for the service of the sanctuary.

As he puts on the goti the priest prays :

May the girdle of faith, which binds my heart and mind, destroy all thoughts of impurity, and may the power of your grace always remain with me; through the grace of our Lord Jesus Christ, to whom glory, power and honour are due, now and forevermore.

As he secures the bazpans :

O Lord, strengthen my hands and wash away all my stains, so that I may serve you with a clean mind and body, through the grace of our Lord Jesus Christ, to whom glory, power and honour are due, now and forevermore.

The varkas is now placed around the priest's neck :

May I receive the yoke of righteousness and may my heart be purged of all sin, through the grace of our Lord Jesus Christ, to whom power, glory and dominion are due now and forevermore.

The choir sings the following, as the schoorchar or cope-like vestment is put on :

Supremely divine and sovereign King of kings, you have robed us, so that we may fittingly serve as ministers of your holy Mysteries.

Priest : Out of your mercy, clothe me with a robe of brightness and by protecting me against the evil designs of the devil may I be considered worthy to praise your glorious Name; through the grace of our Lord Jesus Christ, to whom power, glory and dominion are due, now and forevermore.

As the choir concludes the hymn, the priest says the following prayer :

My soul will joyfully praise the Lord, because he has clothed me in a robe of salvation and a vestment of gladness. He has crowned me like a bridegroom, and like a bride I have been dressed in jewels; through the grace of our Lord Jesus Christ, to whom power, glory and dominion are due now and forevermore.

The choir sings the following at the conclusion of the vesting :

Heavenly King, uphold your Church, and may we worshippers of your holy Name be preserved in peace.

The priest then comes into the middle of the church and proceeds to wash his fingers while reciting Psalm 26:6–12 :

(Kyzord) In innocence I will wash my hands, O Lord, and so I will go to your altar.

(Phokh) O Lord, be my judge, because I have walked innocently. So that thankfully, I may announce and relate your good deeds.

O Lord, how much I love the place where you dwell, the shrine of your glory.

O Lord, never consider this soul-as being lost along with the wicked, nor this life spent among the blood-thirsty, whose hands are always stained with guilt and their palms always ready to accept a bribe.

May my steps be guided clear of wrong, deliver me in your mercy.

My feet are set on sure ground, and where his people congregate there will I join them in blessing the Lord's Name.

Glory be to the Father and to the Son and to the Holy Spirit. As it was in the beginning, is now and shall be forevermore. Amen.

For the sake of the holy mother of God, accept our petitions and save us.

Deacon :   May the holy mother of God and all the saints be intercessors with the Father in heaven, so that mercifully he may save us, his creatures. Almighty God be merciful and save us.

Priest :   Through the pleadings of the holy mother of God, the inviolate mother of your only Son, together with the pleadings of all your saints, may our Lord receive our petitions. Mercifully hear us, pardon, atone and forgive us our sins, so that we may be considered worthy to praise and glorify you, with your Son and the Holy Spirit, now and forevermore. Amen.

The priest bows to the other clergy and says the following confession, while facing the clergy and people :

I confess to almighty God in the sight of the mother of God *(the following, within brackets, is omitted by the Catholic Armenians :)* [who is exalted above all men, in the sight of St John the Fore-runner, St Stephen the Protomartyr, St Gregory the Illuminator, the holy Apostles Peter and Paul] and all the saints, and before you my fathers and brothers, that I have sinned in thought, word and deed, voluntarily and involuntarily, knowingly and through ignorance, that

I have committed all the sins that men commit. Therefore, my brethren, I implore you to pray to the Lord that he might grant me absolution.

The assistant priest replies:

May the almighty and merciful God have mercy upon you, forgive you your sins past and present, and obtain protection for the future. May you receive strength to do good and in the end bring you to life everlasting. Amen.

The priest now turns towards the people and blesses them with a hand cross, saying:

May God, the lover of mankind, deliver you from evil and grant you forgiveness of all your sins. May God give you the opportunity for repentance and the grace to do good. May he, the all-powerful and merciful one, give you the grace of his Holy Spirit, from now and until the end of time, to whom belongs glory now and forevermore. Amen.

Choir : Remember us also, before the immaculate Lamb of God.

The priest, still facing the people, says:

You will be remembered before the immaculate Lamb of God.

During a solemn liturgy two clerics—otherwise the choir—sing Psalm 100, while the deacon prays as below and censes the priest:

Joyfully sing to the Lord, all the earth; serve the Lord gladly.
Enter his presence with exceptional joy.
Know that the Lord is God, and it is he who made us and not we ourselves.
We are his people and the sheep of his pasture.
Enter his gates with praise and his courts with hymns, and give him glory. Praise his name.
Because the Lord is kind and his mercy never ends; his promises will always be fulfilled.
Glory be to the Father and to the Son and to the Holy Spirit. As it was in the beginning, is now and shall be forevermore. Amen.

Deacon : While remembering the patron saints of this church, let us plead to the Lord that he may mercifully assist, preserve and aid us.

As the choir continues to sing Psalm 100, the deacon stops censing the priest as the latter extends his arms and says:

Let us worship at the entrance of the temple. Standing in the sanctuary and approaching the holy and divine Symbols, we bow down in the presence of God, humbly praising the most admirable and triumphant Resurrection *(or Nativity, etc., according to feast being celebrated)* of Christ. Let us therefore offer blessing and glory to the Father and to the Holy Spirit, now and forevermore. Amen.

The ministers now ascend the steps of the altar, saying two verses of Psalm 43 at each step:

Priest :   *(Ktzord)* I will approach the altar of God; to him who is the God of my joy and happiness.

Deacon :   *(Phokh)* Judge me, O God, and defend me against the heathen.
　　　　　　Deliver me from the unjust and dishonest man, because you are my strength, O God.
　　　　　　Why have you cast me aside? And why am I sorrowful while the enemy annoys me?
　　　　　　Send out your light and your truth; they have escorted me in safety to your holy mountain, to the place where you dwell.
　　　　　　And so I will go to the altar of God, to God who is the God of my joy and youthfulness.
　　　　　　To you, O God, I will offer praise upon the harp; why are you sad, O my soul, will you never be at peace?
　　　　　　Wait for God's help; I will never cease to cry out in gratitude, my Champion and my God.
　　　　　　Glory be to the Father and to the Son and to the Holy Spirit. As it was in the beginning, is now and shall be forevermore. Amen.

The Ktzord is repeated again. When the celebrant and the other clergy reach the highest step, the deacon says:

Let us praise God, the Father of our Lord Jesus Christ, who allows us to offer up praise here. O almighty God, save us and have mercy upon us. To you belong power, honour and glory, now and forevermore. Amen.

The priest says the following prayer aloud and with his arms extended:

Bowing before your holy altar in the sanctuary of your holiness, surrounded by angels, the Sacrifice for the atonement of sins and the redemption of the world is offered. In your sanctuary, we offer blessing and glory to you, who live and reign with the Father and the Holy Spirit, now and forevermore, worlds unceasing. Amen.

THE PROTHESIS

If the celebrant is a priest, the curtain is drawn. If a bishop is to celebrate, the two senior deacons each wear the saghavart or priest's cap, and wear the deacon's stole (ourar) crossed in the Byzantine manner; the bishop puts on the pallium and bowing on his knees before the altar, his mitre held above his head by the two deacons, extends his arms and says the following prayers, the first of which is attributed to St Gregory of Narek:

O almighty Lover of mankind, who created everything visible and invisible, Saviour and Guardian, Provider and Peacemaker, Spirit of the Father, we implore you with all our body and soul. We fearfully approach and offer this Sacrifice, first in honour of your inscrutable power, as sharer in the heavenly throne and in its glory with the Father, and as the Searcher, which you are, of the Mysteries of the Father's will, who sent you, as the Saviour and Creator of us all.

It was through you that we learned of the holy Trinity, of which you are one; by you and through you, did the seers of old affirm and prophesy all that was and all that was yet to occur. You, the unlimited force, whom Moses declared to be the Spirit of God moving on the surface of the waters, revealed to us the mystery of regeneration by and through your immense care and consideration for us; who created everything out of nothing, everything that is and was. Every creature which was created by you will be renewed at the resurrection, that day which is the last day of earthly existence and the beginning of our heavenly life.

You, together with the only Son, of the same essence with the Father, obeyed his will unquestioningly. You, the Holy Spirit, he declared as true God, equal and consubstantial with the Father, while you, the Holy Spirit, declared that blasphemy against you would never be forgiven and that you would silence those who were lacking in reverence, while he, the good and holy Saviour of the world, forgave his own accusers, even he who was handed over for our sins and who rose again for our defence. To him be glory; through you and to you, we offer praise with the almighty Father, worlds unceasing. Amen.

The choir, which is also kneeling throughout, sings the following:

You, holy and renowned priest, the elect of God, who are to be compared with Aaron and Moses the prophet, when you enter the sanctuary remember our dead and remember us sinners during the Holy Sacrifice of the altar.

On some occasions, the Prayer of St Gregory of Narek may be repeated; otherwise the bishop may proceed as follows:

Deacon: Father, give the blessing (*Ohrnia der*).

Bishop or celebrant :

> For to you belong clemency, power, love, virtue and glory, forevermore. Amen.
>
> With tears and sorrow, we beg and implore you, the glorious Creator and uncreated, merciful Spirit, our advocate with the Father of mercies, the inspiration of the saints and the purifier of all sinners, release us from every evil deed not in accordance with your will, so that the light of your grace within us will not be extinguished; because we have been taught that it is by prayer and the offering of a good life that we will be united with you. Just as Priest and Victim are one and the same, be pleased to accept our pleadings and prepare a place where we might partake of the Lamb and without condemnation receive the heavenly food, thus securing the foretaste of our salvation.
>
> May all our sins be consumed by the same fire which erased the sins of the prophet, so that in everything your mercy may be seen as the display of the Father's love, shown through the Son, who gave the prodigal son his inheritance and who saved the immoral. Yes, I am a sinner as well; receive me as one who stands in great need of your love. May I be saved by the grace of Christ's redemption, so that in all this the glory of God may be shown to everyone.

As mentioned earlier, during the Matouthsaran or Offertory the veil is drawn, if there is no bishop present ; if a bishop is present, he wears his mitre throughout. On ordinary occasions the priest takes the bread from the deacon and places it upon the paten or maghzmah, while saying :

> In memory of our Lord Jesus Christ, who sits upon a throne not made by man. He offered himself up to the death of the Cross for mankind. Praise, extol and bless him forevermore.

Wine is then taken and poured into the chalice (bashak) in the form of a cross, while the priest says :

> In memory of the life-giving Incarnation of our Lord Jesus Christ, from whose side blood flowed, which regenerated all creation and redeemed mankind. Therefore let us praise and thank him forevermore.

Monophysite Armenians do not add water to the chalice, whereas the Catholics add a little water while the celebrant says the following prayer :

> And one of the soldiers pierced the side of the Creator with a lance, and blood and water flowed.

The priest recites the Prayer of St John Chrysostom :

> O Lord God, who sent our Lord Jesus Christ, the heavenly bread, to be food for the whole world, may he as our saving Redeemer and Benefactor bless and sanctify us. Bless this

Sacrifice and by receiving it at your heavenly altar, may you be pleased to remember your love for mankind, as well as those who offer the Sacrifice and those for whom it is offered.

May we celebrate your holy Mysteries without condemnation, because you are holy and glorious in the most honourable majesty, O Father, Son and Holy Spirit, now and forevermore.

While the priest recites Psalm 92, 'The Lord has reigned and is clothed in beauty', the oblata or srboutheanch are covered with a veil; then a second veil or tsatskoths skih is made to cover the chalice. At the Offertory the choir sings a Meghedi proper to the day:

(*Nativity*) Today a new flower has blossomed from the root of Jesse; a daughter of David has given birth to a son, even the Son of God.

(*Annunciation*) Observe a new truth; Gabriel announces to the pure virgin: 'I am sent to you, O most pure virgin; prepare to receive your Lord.'

(*Transfiguration*) Today a mystic rose of the most beautiful colours crowns the head of the Son of God.

(*Easter*) With all my strength, I will announce him who cried from the Cross, because from the Cross he made his voice to be heard even in the furthermost recesses of limbo.

(*Ascension*) Today the only Son of God as man, even as a son of Adam, ascended into heaven and today choirs of angels sing hymns of praise.

(*Pentecost*) Today let us sing hymns of praise to the Holy Spirit, and with dignity let us rejoice in the renewal of everything.

(*Feast of the Apostles*) The Son of righteousness, who proceeds from the Father, has filled you, O holy Apostles, with ineffable grace and glorious light, and has illuminated the Armenian nation, through the efforts of the glorious Thaddeus and the holy Bartholomew.

At the conclusion of the seasonal or festal Meghedi, the Hymn of Censing, which appears below, is sung by the choir. Meanwhile the oblata are censed three times by the priest or celebrant:

May the Holy Spirit descend upon you, and may the power of almighty God overshadow you.

At the conclusion of the foregoing and the recitation of Psalm 93, the curtain is drawn back, and the altar, the crucifix, the oblata, the clergy, choir and people are all incensed. The choir sings the Hymn of Censing:

In this place of sacrifice in the house of the Lord, we who are gathered together to celebrate the Mysteries, compose a choir of sweet perfume. Favourably accept our prayers as the perfume of sweet-smelling incense, myrrh and cinnamon. May we be able to persevere in our resolve to serve you always; accept the petitions of your ministers, through the pleadings of your virgin mother.

During the censing of the altar, oblata and congregation, the priest recites this prayer:

O Lord Jesus Christ, to you we offer sweet perfumed incense; may it ascend to you in heaven and be acceptable to you. Pour down upon us, we implore you, the grace of the Holy Spirit, because to you, with the Father and the Holy Spirit, we attribute glory, now and forevermore. Amen.

At the conclusion of the prayer, the priest, accompanied by the deacon(s), descends the altar steps and incenses the people. If a bishop is the celebrant, he processes into the nave of the church, accompanied by his clergy, some of whom may carry keshotz and thuribles, to assist in the incensing of the church and its furnishings. During the censing, the choir continues the Hymn of Censing:

With Christ's blood the Church has been made more illustrious than heaven, and following the pattern of the heavenly armies you have provided orders of apostles, prophets and holy teachers. We priests, deacons, readers and clergy gathered here burn incense before you, just as Zacharias did. Accept our prayers which we offer with the incense, like the sacrifices of Abel, Noah and Abraham.

The choir then sings the Hymn of the Church:

O Zion, daughter of light, O holy Church, rejoice. Beautify yourself, O bride of Christ and heavenlike sanctuary, in preparation for the anointed God who is sacrificed within you and who gives his own body and blood in accordance with his own command. May he forgive the sins of this church's founders. The holy Church acknowledges the pure virgin Mary, mother of God, from whom we have received the bread of life and the cup of happiness. With hymns, let us bless the Lord.

The celebrant returns to the altar, incenses it again and kisses it. Meanwhile the senior deacon stands either in the middle of the church or by the side of the altar and says:

Father, give the blessing.

Priest: Blessed be the kingdom of the Father, the Son and the Holy Spirit, now and forevermore. Amen.

*Among the Dissident Armenians, the following Hymn or Shammamout, 'O
only Son . . .', follows, whereas among the Uniate or Catholic Armenians
an Introit follows, which is proper to the feast or Sunday. The Hymn 'O
only Son . . .' is sung on ordinary Sundays of the year and on the commemoration of the Nativity.*

Choir :   O only Son and Word of God, save us; born of the virgin
            Mary, you became man and were crucified and overcame
            death by your death. You, being one of the holy Trinity,
            are glorified with the Father and the Holy Spirit.

Deacon :   Again and again, let us implore the Lord in peace to merci-
            fully receive and save us. Father, give the blessing.

The priest gives the blessing with a hand cross :

            Blessing and glory be to the Father, the Son and the Holy
            Spirit, now and forevermore. Amen. Peace be ✠ with you
            all.

Choir :   And with you.

*The deacons then arrange themselves on either side of the altar, while the
senior deacon says :*

            Let us adore the Lord.

Choir :   Before you, O Lord.

*The priest raises and extends his hands and with a loud voice says the prayer
of the First Antiphon :*

            O Lord our God, whose glory, power and mercy are im-
            measurable, look upon us and this holy church in your great
            love and show us and those who pray with us the extent of
            your mercies and sympathy, because to you belong glory,
            power and honour, now and forevermore. Amen.

*The choir now sings the following, which is one of eight alternatives ap-
pointed for ordinary Sundays of the year :*

            The Lord is king and has been clothed in glorious robes.
            Christ, who is the king, became man of the virgin Mary and
            is consubstantial with the Father.
                Let glory be given to you, O Christ the king of glory, who
            by voluntarily dying overcame death and by whose glorious
            resurrection the world was renewed.
                May glory be given to you, O Christ the king of glory.
                Glory be to the Father and to the Son and to the Holy
            Spirit. As it was in the beginning, is now and shall be forever-
            more.
                With the angels we sing to you, O Christ, the king of
            glory, who enlightened the Church; may glory be given to
            you.

During the previous hymn, the priest says this prayer in a low voice:

> O Lord our God, save your people and bless your heritage; preserve the integrity of your Church and sanctify those who reverently love the majesty of your house. May they be rewarded with your divine power and may they who hope in you never be abandoned.

The priest gives the following blessing without facing the people:

> Peace ✠ be with you all. O God, who promised us, by your grace, that whenever two or more have gathered together in your name you will grant them their requests, grant the wishes and pleas of your servants. O Lord, may we receive in this world knowledge of your truth and in the next world life everlasting. Because you are beneficent and full of love, all glory, power and honour are due to you. Amen.

The priest extends his arms and continues in a low voice:

> O Lord God, who established in heaven the armies of angels and archangels for the service of your glory, may our entrance now be accompanied by an entrance of holy angels ministering with us and glorifying your goodness.

Deacon :   Father, give us a blessing.

Priest :   For yours is the kingdom the power and the glory, now and forevermore. Amen.

The priest then kisses the altar.

MASS OF THE CATECHUMENS

Deacon :   Proschumen *(Let us be attentive).*

During the chanting of the Trisagion or Ereshsrbeann which follows, the Book of Gospels is carried in procession around the altar by the deacons, accompanied by keshotz, a thurifer and clerics holding tapers. The thurifer incenses the book continuously. When the procession has returned to the altar, the Book of Gospels is given by the thurifer to the senior chorister or layman, who kisses it, while the priest blesses him. Sometimes the priest will simply bless the congregation with the book. The choir sings three times:

> Holy God, Holy and Strong, Holy and Immortal, have mercy upon us.

Dissident Armenians recite a different Trisagion; the form which was once acceptable to the Catholic Armenians has since been considered unacceptable. The dissident version reads:

> Holy God, Holy and Strong, Holy and Immortal, (who rose from the dead), have mercy upon us.

This is sung three times, and according to the feast the words in quotes as follows: Nativity, 'who came to live among us'; Ascension, 'who ascended into heaven with great glory'; Transfiguration, 'who were transfigured among men'; Holy Saturday, 'who were buried'. During the procession of the Book of Gospels, the priest recites the following prayer of the Trisagion in a low voice:

> O Holy God, reposing in the Holy of Holies, you are praised and glorified by the seraphim and cherubim and adored by all the powers of heaven. You have created everything that is, and in your likeness you have created man, to whom you have given all your graces. You have taught man to look for wisdom and knowledge and you did not disregard the sinner, but through repentance you saved him.
>
> You have allowed us, your worthless and humble servants, to stand before you in the glory of your holy altar to offer worship and suitable praise. Accept the hymn of the Trisagion, O Lord, and out of your goodness preserve us. Forgive us all our sins, voluntarily and involuntarily committed; make our hearts and bodies holy and grant that we may faithfully serve you for the rest of our lives, through the intercessions of the holy mother of God, together with all the saints, who have pleased you, since the creation of the world.

Priest, in a loud voice:

> Because You are holy, O God, and to you we attribute all honour and power, now and forevermore. Amen.

THE LITANY

Deacon :   Again and again, let us peacefully implore the Lord.

Choir :   Lord, have mercy upon us *(Der Oghormia)*.

Deacon :   Let us ask the Lord for the peace of the world and for the stability of the Church.

Choir :   Lord, have mercy upon us.

Deacon :   Let us implore the Lord for all holy and orthodox bishops.

Choir :   Lord have mercy upon them.

Deacon :   For our Holy Father, Pope N., for the Patriarch N., let us implore the Lord.

Choir :   Lord, preserve them and have mercy upon them.

Deacon :   For all vartapets, priests, deacons, singers and all your people, let us implore the Lord.

Choir :   Lord, preserve them and have mercy upon them.

Deacon :   For all pious kings and their families, their generals and their defence forces, let us implore the Lord.

Choir :   Lord, mercifully protect them.

Deacon :   For those who have died in the faith of Christ let us implore the Lord.

Choir :   Lord, remember them and have mercy upon them.

Deacon :   Again and again, let us pray for the unity of our true and holy faith.

Choir :   Lord, have mercy upon us.

Deacon :   Let us commend ourselves to the Lord God Almighty.

Choir :   We will devote ourselves to you, O Lord.

Deacon :   With one accord, let us say: out of your great mercy, have pity on us, O Lord our God.

Choir :   Lord, have mercy upon us *(three times)*.

During the Litany, the priest lifts and extends his hands and says the following in a low voice :

O Lord God, accept this sincere prayer of your servants and out of the greatness of your mercy pity us and be merciful to us all who have put our confidence in the immensity of your mercy.

Deacon :   Father, give the blessing.

Priest :   For you are a merciful God and a Lover of mankind; to you we attribute honour, power and glory, now and forevermore. Amen.

The priest then kisses the altar and sits down. If the celebrant is a bishop, he will go to his throne and remain there with his deacons until after the conclusion of the Gospel. Meanwhile the choir sings the Saghmos Jashou or Psalm before the Prophecy, which varies according to the Season. The Prophecy is then read, after which the choir will sing the Mesedi or Psalm before the Epistle (this term also refers to the Hymn sung at Vespers). The Epistle or Arrachealch is read and at its conclusion, as at the conclusion of every Lesson, the choir sings : Alleluia. When the priest has blessed the deacon and the incense, he turns towards the people and blesses them as follows :

Deacon :   Stand up.

Priest, blessing with a hand cross :

Peace ✠ be with you all.

Choir :   And   with   you.

Deacon :   Listen with fear.

The deacon who is to read the Gospel says :

     The holy Gospel according to N.

Choir :   Glory be to you, O Lord our God.

Deacon :   Let us be attentive *(Proschumen)*.

Choir :   God speaks.

During the recitation of the Gospel, the senior deacon stands at the north side of the altar, on the top step, while the priest stands facing the altar and still wearing his cap; among dissident Armenians, it is usual to remove the saghavart. The Gospel is chanted by a deacon, who faces the congregation, while in front of him on a lower step another deacon stands holding a censer, with which he incenses the Book of Gospels at the conclusion of every sentence. The deacon chanting the Gospel is flanked on either side by two minor clerics bearing lighted tapers. At the conclusion of the Gospel the choir says :

     Glory be to you, O Lord our God.

The priest then stands in front of the altar and recites the Creed, while the deacon, standing alongside the priest and holding the Book of the Gospels, repeats the Creed. During the recitation of the Creed, the clergy and people are incensed. During a pontifical liturgy, the bishop comes to the altar for the recitation of the Creed, but returns to the throne before the commencement of the Litany which follows it.

THE CREED

The text of the Creed or Khavatamch which follows is as it was after the Second Council of Constantinople, except for the additions which appear in parentheses and which are explained in italics :

     We believe in one God, the Father Almighty, Maker of heaven and earth, of things visible and invisible. And in one Lord Jesus Christ, the Son of God, begotten of God the Father (of the very Essence of the Father; *this was inserted against the Arians*), God of God, Light of Light, very God of very God, an offspring and not of a thing made, of the very Nature of the Father, by whom all things, both visible and invisible, were made in heaven and upon earth, who for us men and for our salvation came down from heaven and was incarnate and was made man (perfectly begotten; *against the Apollinarians*) by the Holy Spirit of the most holy virgin Mary (he assumed from her flesh, soul and mind and all things that are in man, truly and not figuratively; *against the Gnostics*), who having suffered, been crucified and buried, rose again the third day ascending into heaven (in the same body; *against the Gnostics*) and sat down at the right hand of the Father; he shall come again (in the same body; *against the Gnostics*) in the glory of the Father to judge the living and the dead; his kingdom shall have no end.

We also believe in the Holy Spirit, uncreated and most perfect, who proceeded from the Father and the Son, who spoke in the Law, in the Prophets and in the Gospel; who descended upon Jordan, who announced him that was sent, and who dwells among the saints.

We also believe in one, holy, catholic and apostolic church; in one baptism; in penance for the expiation and remission of sins; in the resurrection of the dead and eternal judgment both of souls and bodies; in the kingdom of heaven and in everlasting life.

The Anathema which follows was found in the Creed of St Gregory of Tours, and dates from the late sixth century :

And as regards them who say there was a time when the Son of Man was not, or, in like manner, there was a time when the Holy Spirit was not, or that they were made of nothing or that the Son of God and the Holy Spirit are of another substance, or that they are changeable, the Orthodox and Apostolic Church says: let them be anathema.

The deacon now hands the Book of Gospels to the priest, saying :

Father, give the blessing.

The priest then kisses the Book of Gospels and says the Confession of St Gregory :

And we adore him who was before all time; we worship the Holy Trinity, God the Father, the Son and the Holy Spirit, now and forevermore. Amen.

During the Litany which follows, the priest, with his arms raised up and extended, silently says the Prayer for the Gifts :

O Lord Jesus Christ, our Saviour, merciful and generous in the conferring of your favours, you endured, at this time, the torments and death of the Cross for our sins and granted the holy Apostles the gifts of the Holy Spirit; we implore you to allow us to share in your heavenly gifts, for the remission of our sins and the reception of the same Holy Spirit.

During the recitation of this prayer, the deacon commences the Litany.

Deacon :   Again and again, let us peacefully implore the Lord.

Choir :   Lord, have mercy.

Deacon :   Again and again, let us pray with faith at this time of sacrifice, and ask the Lord God, our Saviour Jesus Christ, that he would graciously accept and listen to our pleas and that our petitions may be favourably received, so that our sins may mercifully be pardoned; that he would always allow our prayers and pleadings to ascend before his divine majesty, so that he would grant us the grace to continue to do good and to persevere in the faith. May almighty God mercifully pour out his grace upon us and save us. Have mercy upon us.

Choir :   O Lord, save us.

Deacon :   Let us implore the Lord to allow us to spend today and this hour of sacrifice peacefully.

Choir :   O Lord, grant this request.

Deacon :   Let us pray to the Lord for the angel of peace and the guardian of our souls.

Choir :   O Lord, grant this request.

Deacon :   Let us pray to the Lord for the pardon of our sins.

Choir :   O Lord, grant this request.

Deacon :   Let us pray to the Lord, that he might send us the great and victorious peace of his most holy Cross.

Choir :   O Lord, grant this request.

Deacon :   Again let us pray for the unity of our true and holy faith.

Choir :   Lord, have mercy.

Deacon :   We will all devote ourselves and one another to you, O Lord God almighty.

Choir :   We will devote ourselves to you, O Lord.

Deacon :   Let us all say together: O God, out of your great mercy, pity us.

Choir :   Lord, have mercy (three times).

Deacon :   Father, give the blessing.

Priest :   So that we may be made worthy to adore you with thanks, with the Father and the Holy Spirit, now and forevermore. Amen. Peace ✠ be with you all.

Choir :   And with you.

Deacon :   Let us pray to the Lord.

Choir :   Before you, O Lord.

Priest :   O Christ our Saviour, through your grace which is beyond all understanding may we be preserved from the fear of evil. Grant us, along with all your faithful, the grace to worship you in spirit and in truth, because all glory, power and honour belong to the most holy Trinity, now and forevermore, worlds unceasing.

Choir :   Amen.

Priest :   Blessed be our Lord Jesus Christ.

Choir :   Amen.

Deacon :   Father, give the blessing.

Priest :   The Lord our God ✠ bless you all.

Choir :   Amen.

This blessing before the dismissal of the catechumens is also found in the Greek liturgy. While the priest then says in silence the Prayer of the Great Entrance, the choir and deacon continue to sing the following :

Deacon :   May neither the catechumens, nor the penitents who have not been purified, nor those of little faith be allowed to approach these divine Mysteries.

Choir :   The body and blood of our Saviour are about to be before us. The heavenly armies, invisible to us, sing unceasingly: 'Holy, Holy, Holy, Lord God of hosts.'

Dissident Armenians substitute the following :

Choir :   The body of our Lord and the blood of our Saviour are before us. The heavenly armies, invisible to us, sing unceasingly: 'Holy, Holy, Holy, Lord God of hosts.'

Deacon :   O Choirs, sing psalms and hymns to the Lord our God.

The curtain is then closed and the celebrant takes off his saghavart and places it upon the altar. If a bishop is the celebrant, he takes off his emiphoron, mitre and pastoral staff. It should be noted that until now the bishop has blessed the people with a hand cross, but from now on he will bless with his hands only, whereas the priest continues to bless with the hand cross. The curtain is re-opened and the choir sings a hymn, which varies according to the season. During Paschaltide :

What lord is like our God? He has even been crucified for us. He was buried and rose again and has been recognized as God by the whole world, and has ascended to heaven with glory. Come, let us sing praises to him and with all the army of heaven let us say: Holy, Holy, Holy, O Lord our God.

Dissident Armenians use the following hymn at Easter :

Let us, who mystically represent the cherubim and who sing hymns to the holy Trinity, leave aside all our worldly cares so that we may receive the King of glory, who is attended by all the angelic armies. Alleluia. Alleluia. Alleluia.

On Sundays and feasts:

Even though you have created the heavenly armies to adore you in your Church and countless numbers of archangels and angels to offer service to you, nevertheless you are pleased to receive praise from mortal men with these words: Holy, Holy, Holy, Lord God of hosts.

During the singing of these hymns the Great Entrance is made, while the people kneel. The senior deacon incenses the altar nine times and bows three times. Then in company with another deacon he proceeds to the credence table on the right-hand side of the altar, where the gifts are incensed. The censer is then given to another deacon or cleric. A deacon takes the chalice upon which rests the paten holding the bread, the whole being covered with a veil; he raises it to the level of his head and carries it around the back of the altar, from north to south. Fans, carried by other clerics, are waved and together with tapers and incense the procession comes to the front of the altar, where the priest has been praying the Prayer of the Great Entrance. Where there is no deacon, the priest himself performs the Great Entrance.

THE PRAYER OF THE GREAT ENTRANCE

The priest bows and says this prayer in a very low voice:

None of us who are bound by the demands of the senses are worthy to come before your holy altar, nor to offer sacrifice to you, the King of glory, because to serve you is an awesome undertaking, even for the heavenly powers themselves. But through your unspeakable and boundless love, you became man without undergoing any change and assumed the title of our high priest. You who are the Lord of all gave us the priesthood for this holy ministry and you gave us this unbloody Sacrifice, because you are the Lord our God, who rules over everything both in heaven and earth.

To you who sit between the cherubim and seraphim and live in the Holy of Holies and are the true King of Israel and who alone are holy and remain in the company of the saints, we address our pleas.

You who alone are good and ready to listen, look upon me a sinner and unworthy servant. Purify my heart and soul from an evil conscience and through the power of the Holy Spirit may my resolutions be strengthened, even I who have received the grace of your priesthood, so that I may stand before your holy altar and consecrate your immaculate body and precious blood.

Humbly bowing my head before you, I approach and implore you not to disregard nor reject me from the number of your servants, but allow me, a sinner, your unworthy servant, to offer these gifts to you.

The priest then turns towards the deacon and censes the gifts which the deacon still holds. The priest then takes the chalice and disk, still covered with the veil, and places the gifts upon the altar. Again he incenses them and elevates them towards the cross. A deacon then fetches water in preparation for the Lavabo, before which the priest concludes the Prayer of the Great Entrance:

Because you are both priest and victim, he who receives and is received, to you, O Christ our God, we attribute honour, power and glory, now and forevermore. Amen.

The priest now washes his hands while reciting the Lavabo (Psalm 26:6–12). He then recites the Prayer of St Athanasius of Alexandria, while the deacon says:

Deacon :   Again and again, let us implore the Lord in peace.

Choir :   Lord, have mercy upon us.

Deacon :   Full of faith and holiness, let us stand before God's holy table and may we not pray proudly, deceitfully, maliciously or with any doubt, but may our prayers be accompanied by a pure intention and a clean heart and with a perfectly charitable faith.
              Prayerfully let us stand before the holy altar of God, and so we will find grace and mercy on the last day, when everything will be revealed at the second coming of our Lord Jesus Christ, who will save and have mercy upon us.

Choir :   O Lord, mercifully save us.

The Prayer of St Athanasius of Alexandria

The priest raises and extends his hands, while saying in a low voice:

O Lord God of hosts, who created everything and permitted us dull creatures to be ministers of this awesome and fearful Mystery; O Lord to whom we present this sacrifice, accept this offering from us and make it the Mystery of the body and blood of your only Son. Grant that the bread and wine which we will receive, will heal and pardon.

Deacon :   Father, give the blessing.

Priest :   Through the grace and love of our Lord and Saviour Jesus Christ *(the priest kisses the altar)* to whom we attribute all honour, power and glory, now and forevermore, worlds unceasing.

Choir :   Amen.

The Kiss of Peace
(Hampuir Srboutian)

The priest, facing the people :

Peace ✠ be with you all.

Choir :   And with you.

Deacon :   Let us adore the Lord.

Choir :   Before you, O Lord.

Deacon :   Greet one another with a holy kiss; let those who are unable to participate, retire outside the doors and pray there.

The priest kisses the altar. He is then censed by the deacon, who also kisses the altar and then the arms of the celebrant. The deacon then conveys the kiss to the clergy and choir, who kiss shoulders. Meanwhile the choir sings the following :

Christ has appeared among us, and when he is present the voice of peace should be heard; we have been ordered to perform this holy greeting. All hatred has been taken away and love should prevail everywhere. Now all you ministers, raise your voices in unison and bless the consubstantial godhead, who is adored by the seraphim.

The priest then kisses the altar again, and each member of the congregation places his hand over his heart and bows to his neighbour. On solemn feast days, the following is substituted for the hymn sung by the choir.

Deacon :   You, who with faith surround this sacred and royal altar, look upon Christ the King, seated there surrounded by the heavenly hosts.

Choir :   With our eyes towards heaven let us pray, saying: Do not remember our sins but in your clemency pardon us. We bless you; with the angels and with the saints, we say: Glory to you, O Lord.

Otherwise the deacon says :

Fearfully, let us stand up and humbly pay attention.

Choir :   Before you, O Lord.

Deacon :   Christ the immaculate Lamb of God has offered himself as the victim.

Choir :   Mercy and peace and the sacrifice of praise.

Deacon :   Father, give the blessing.

THE ANAPHORA

(Attributed to St Athanasius)

The priest, with hand cross :

> The grace ✠ of the love and of the divine sanctifying power
> of the Father, the Son and the Holy Spirit be with you all.

Choir :   And with you.

Deacon :   Guard the doors with all wisdom and caution. Fearfully let
us lift up our hearts.

*The reference to the doors is of course quite archaic and refers to the caution
that used to be maintained in ensuring that no catechumen remained for this
solemn part of the liturgy.*

Choir :   We lift them up to you, O Lord God almighty.

Deacon :   O Lord, with all our hearts, let us give thanks to you.

Choir :   It is right and reasonable to do so.

*During the foregoing prayers, the priest, in a low voice and with clasped
hands, has been reciting the prayer which appears below.*

> It is truly just and reasonable that we should always devoutly
> worship and adore you, almighty Father, who with the co-
> operation of your incomprehensible Word destroyed the
> bonds of the curse, because he has gathered together those
> who believe in you and has formed a Church, which you
> have claimed for yourself. He condescended to live among
> us as a human, which nature he took from the virgin Mary,
> and by a new act as God, created a heaven upon earth.
>
> God, before whom even the angels could not stand on
> account of the splendour of his divinity, became man for
> the sake of our salvation and has enabled us to participate
> with the hosts of heaven in forming a spiritual choir.

On some feasts, the following is added by the deacon :

> O Christ, we give you thanks at all times and everywhere for
> our salvation, through which the heavenly host praise your
> glorious *(Resurrection, Ascension, etc.)*, the seraphim tremble,
> the cherubim shudder and the awesome powers of heaven
> form a choir and shout with joy saying:

Deacon :   Father, give the blessing.

The priest, aloud :

> And with the cherubim and seraphim to boldly and confidently sing the sacred Hymn.

Choir :   Holy, Holy, Holy. You are the Lord God of the heavenly hosts. Heaven and earth resound with your glory. Hosanna in the highest. Blessed are you, who come in the name of the Lord. Hosanna in the highest.

While the choir sing the Hymn 'Holy, Holy, Holy', the assistant clergy kneel and the fans are shaken, while the priest extends his arms and silently recites the following prayer :

> Holy, Holy, Holy. Truly you are the most holy. Who is there who can describe the gift that flows down upon us unceasingly? Because you protected and comforted our ancestors in many ways by prophecies, by the law, the priesthood and the sacrifice of oxen, which was a foreshadow of that which was to come. And when finally he did come, you destroyed our sins and gave us your only Son, the debtor and the debt, the Sacrifice and the Anointed, the Lamb and the Bread of heaven, the Priest and the Victim, because it is he who gives and he who is always inexhaustibly given to us. Truly he was man by a union without fusion and was born of the mother of God, the virgin Mary, and in everything except sin lived as man. He was the saviour of the world and the cause of our salvation.

Deacon :   Father, give the blessing.

The thurifer, having finished censing the ministers collectively, kneels on the first step of the altar. The priest then kisses the altar and taking up the bread in his hands, says in a low voice :

> Then taking the bread in his holy, divine, immaculate and venerable hands, he blessed ✠ it, gave thanks, broke it and gave to his holy disciples seated at table with him, saying:

In a loud voice :

> Take and eat, this is my Body, which is given for you and for many, for the expiation and remission of sins.

Choir :   Amen.

During the consecration, the priest holds the host and chalice at the level of his head. The priest then lowers his voice as he places his hands on the chalice and continues :

> Similarly, he also took the cup; he blessed ✠ it and having given thanks he drank and gave it to his holy and chosen disciples while they were seated at table with him, saying:
> *(the priest raises his voice as he continues) :*

Deacon :   Father, give the blessing.

The priest, aloud :

> Drink all of this; this is my blood of the New Testament which is shed for you and for many for the expiation and remission of sins.

Choir :   Amen.

The celebrant usually makes a simple bow, while the deacon or thurifer censes the sacrament and the fans are shaken. The choir sings :

> O heavenly Father, who gave your Son as a debtor of our debts, we implore you, for the sake of his blood, which has flowed for us, to have mercy upon us, your rational flock.

Meanwhile the priest recites the following prayer in a low voice with his arms partially extended :

> And your only Son, the lover of mankind, commanded us to do this in memory of him. When he descended into the grave, with the body he had assumed, victoriously he destroyed the gates of hell, and showed you to us as the one true God, the God of both the living and the dead.

The priest then takes the oblation in his hands, and makes the sign of the cross with both the host and the chalice, while continuing in a low voice :

> Therefore now, O Lord, in obedience to your command, we perform this Mystery of the body and blood of your only Son and remember his sufferings on account of our sins, his crucifixion, which he endured while still alive, the burial for three days, his holy resurrection and ascension and his session at your right hand, O Father. We also confirm and bless his awesome and glorious Second Coming again.

Deacon :   Father, give the blessing.

The priest then raises the oblations and replaces them upon the altar and continues aloud :

> We offer to you your own gifts, in all and for all.

Choir :   In everything, you are blessed, O Lord; we sing to you and address our prayers to you, O our God.

While the choir sings this, the priest raises his hands and with his arms open, he secretly says the following :

> Truly, O Lord God, we sing to you and will always give thanks to you, because you have not despised our unworthiness to participate in this awesome and ineffable Mystery, but you have appointed us as its ministers, not on account of

our good deeds, because these have always been conspicuously absent, but confident of your immense mercy, we dare to draw near to the administration of the body and blood of your only Son, our Lord and Saviour Jesus Christ, to whom belong glory, dominion and honour, now and forevermore, worlds unceasing. Amen.

Deacon : Father give the blessing.

The priest turns to face the people :

Peace ✠ be with you all.

Choir : And with you.

Deacon : Let us adore God.

Choir : Before you, O Lord.
O Lord, the Son of God, who was sacrificed to the Father for our atonement, because you are the bread of life given to us, we implore you, by the shedding of your precious blood, that you might have mercy upon your flock, which you have redeemed.

The priest then bows very low and in a low voice commences the Epiclesis, during which the thurifer censes the oblata :

We worship, pray and implore you, O God of mercy, that you would send down on us and upon this offering, which we present to you, your holy consubstantial Spirit *(the priest blesses the host)* ✠ by whose operation you have truly made this holy bread the body of our Lord *(this is said three times)*.

The priest then blesses the chalice three times, saying each time :

✠ By whose operation also, you have truly made that which is in the chalice the blood of our Lord Jesus Christ.

The priest then blesses both species together, saying three times :

✠ By whose operation you have truly made the holy bread and wine the body and blood of our Lord Jesus Christ, in transforming them by the Holy Spirit.

At each blessing the deacon says : Amen. *Finally, the priest elevates the sacred species, saying :*

May this be to us who receive it, not for our condemnation, but for a cleansing and remission of our sins.

The deacon now incenses the sacrament, the assistant clergy and congregation, while the choir sings the following hymn :

O Spirit of God, who descended from heaven, we implore you to perform through our hands the Mystery of the

Sacrament of him who is glorified with you. By the shedding of his blood, we beg you to give rest to our dead brethren.

The priest makes the following commemorations in a low voice, while keeping his hands lowered, but not extended over the oblations.

PRAYER FOR THE LIVING

By this sacrifice send down upon us the charity, stability and world peace which we desire. Extend your peace also to the Church, to all Orthodox bishops, priests and deacons, kings, princes and people, and to all who are travelling, to those in captivity or who are in any way distressed, to those who are at war with barbarians. Through this sacrifice may we obtain favourable weather and the fruitfulness of the earth, and may the sick speedily recover from their ailments.

PRAYER FOR THE DEAD

By this sacrifice may rest be given to the patriarchs, the teachers, the prophets, apostles and martyrs; to all bishops, priests, deacons and clergy, together with all your Church and all the faithful, both men and women, who have died in the faith of your holy Church.

Deacon :   Father, give the blessing.

The priest, aloud :

O merciful and beneficient God, we implore you to come among us.

Choir :   Remember, O Lord, and have mercy upon us.

Priest :   We pray that the holy mother of God, the ever virgin Mary, together with John the Baptist, the first confessor St Stephen and all the saints, may be remembered in this holy Sacrifice.

Choir :   Remember, O Lord, and have mercy upon us.

During the Litany which follows, the priest says the following prayer privately :

PRAYER FOR THE CHURCH

Remember, O Lord, bless and have mercy upon your holy catholic and apostolic Church, which you redeemed with the precious blood of your only Son. By his sacrifice upon the Cross, may the Church be granted an eternal peace, O Lord. Remember and give your blessing to all Orthodox bishops who have correctly taught us the truth.

THE LITANY

The deacons then retire to the right-hand side of the altar; with clasped hands, the senior deacon says the following:

> We pray that all holy apostles, prophets, vartapets, martyrs and all holy popes, apostolic bishops, priests, orthodox deacons and all the saints, may be remembered in this holy Sacrifice.

Choir : Remember, O Lord, and have mercy upon us.

Deacon, on ordinary Sundays:

> Let us give thanks for the blessed, praised, glorious and admirable *(Resurrection, Ascension)* of Christ *(or descent of the Holy Spirit).*

Choir : Glory be to you, O *(risen, ascended)* Christ.

Otherwise, on saints' days, the deacon says:

> We pray that Saint N. whose memory is celebrated today may be commemorated in this holy Sacrifice.

Choir : Remember, O Lord, and have mercy upon us.

In the prayer which follows, the Dissident Armenians insert the names of John of Odsenti, Gregory and Moses of Tathivan, following the commemoration of Nierces of Klaen.

Deacons : We pray that our first preachers and illuminators, the holy apostles Thaddeus and Bartholomew, our first patriarch and illuminator Gregory, the saints Aristaces, Vertannes, Oscan, Gregory, Nierces, Isaac, Daniel, Khath, Mesrop the Teacher, Gregory of Narighon, Nierces of Klaen, Gregory and Nierces and all the saints, together with all holy Armenian fathers, pastors and teachers, may be commemorated in this holy Sacrifice.

Choir : Remember, O Lord, and have mercy upon us.

Among the Dissidents, the response is: 'Remember, O Lord; have mercy upon them'.

Deacon : Let us pray that the holy recluses, our venerable and God-fearing religious, Paul, Anthony, Polus, Macarius, Onophrius, Mark the Abbot, Seraphion, Nilus, Arsenius, Evagrius, John, Simon, Oski and his companions, Sukias and his companions, together with all holy and venerable fathers and their followers throughout the world, may be remembered in this holy Sacrifice.

Choir : Remember, O Lord, and have mercy upon us.

Deacon :   We pray and remember in this holy Sacrifice the faithful kings and saints, Abgar, Constantine, Tiridates and Theodosius, together with all pious kings and princes.

Choir :   Remember, O Lord, and have mercy upon us.

All the deacons then gather together in front of the altar and chant the following :

> Let us pray that all believers, men and women, old and young of every age, who have died in holiness, in the faith of Christ, may be remembered in this holy Sacrifice.

Choir :   Remember them, O Lord, and have mercy upon us.

During these commemorations, the priest says the following in a low voice :

> Remember, O Lord, and have mercy and bless your holy catholic and apostolic Church, which you ransomed with the precious blood of your only Son and delivered by the power of the holy Cross; grant it a strong and definite peace. Remember, O Lord, and have mercy and bless all Orthodox bishops, who have preached the true doctrine of Christ.

All the deacons then gather at the epistle side of the altar and say :

> Father, bless.

The priest, aloud :

> Maintain our holy Father Pope N. in the true doctrine for many years, together with our venerable Patriarch N. and the Ordinary of the diocese N.

Then the protodeacon or senior deacon, at the left-hand side of the altar, sings the following prayer :

> We offer to you, O Lord our God, our thanks and praise for the most holy and immortal Sacrifice, which is now on this holy table. May it sanctify our lives and give charity, strength of purpose and peace to us, to the whole world, to the holy Church, to all Orthodox bishops, particularly our Holy Father Pope N., our venerable Patriarch N. and to the priest who offers this Sacrifice. Give strength and victory to all Christian kings and princes. We also implore and pray to you for the souls of those who have died, our teachers, the founders of this church and those buried nearby in the churchyard. We also pray for the release of those in prison, for the health of all those present here, and for the eternal rest of those who have died in the faith; we implore you that they may be remembered in this holy Sacrifice.

Choir :   In all and for all.

The priest meanwhile, in a low voice, says the Prayer of the People :

Remember, O Lord, and have mercy upon your people who stand here before you and upon him who offers this Sacrifice and grant what is necessary and good for them. Remember, O Lord, bless and have mercy upon the pious, who bring gifts to your holy Church and who remember the poor in their almsgiving. Whatever they have given you, may they receive it back a hundred times over.

Remember, O Lord, and demonstrate your mercy and pity on the souls of the dead; may they rest in peace together with your saints in heaven, and may they be made worthy of your mercy.

Remember, O Lord, the soul of your servant N. *(the benefactor of the church is mentioned)* ; out of the immensity of your great kindness, have mercy upon him, and may he joyfully see the light of your glory. *(If the benefactor is still alive, the following is substituted : May he be guarded from all spiritual and bodily ills.)*

Remember, O Lord, all those who have asked us to remember them, whether alive or dead. May their wills and ours be directed in the path of salvation, and may all men receive the benefits of your great and inexhaustible mercy. Purify our thoughts and make us worthy to receive the body and blood of your only Son, our Lord and Saviour Jesus Christ, to whom with you, almighty Father, together with the Holy Spirit, belong all glory, dominion and honour, now and forevermore, worlds unceasing. Amen.

Deacon :   Father, give the blessing.

The priest half turns towards the people :

And the mercy of our great God and Saviour Jesus Christ be with ✠ you all.

Choir :   And with you.

Deacon :   Again and again, let us pray to the Lord for peace.

Choir :   Lord, have mercy upon us.

Deacon :   Together with all the saints we have commemorated, let us pray to the Lord.

Choir :   Lord, have mercy upon us.

Deacon :   Let us pray to the Lord for all those who offer this holy and divine Sacrifice which is lying upon this altar.

Choir :   Lord, have mercy upon us.

Deacon :   Let us pray that the Lord our God, the lover of mankind, will accept this Sacrifice as a sweet-smelling perfume and that he will send down upon us his heavenly grace and the gift of his Holy Spirit.

Choir :   Lord, have mercy upon us.

Deacon :   Assist, preserve, comfort and guard us, O Lord God. May he have mercy upon us.

Choir :   Save us, O Lord, and have mercy upon us.

Deacon :   Lord, have mercy upon us, who have remembered the most holy mother of God, the ever virgin Mary and all the saints.

Choir :   Lord, have mercy upon us.

Deacon :   Let us pray to the Lord for the unity of our true and holy faith.

Choir :   Lord, have mercy upon us.

Deacon :   Let us offer our souls and all that we have to the Lord God almighty.

Choir :   O Lord, we offer ourselves to you.

Deacon :   Together let us say: out of your great kindness, have mercy upon us, O Lord our God.

Choir :   Lord, have mercy upon us *(three times)*.

During the foregoing, the priest has been silently praying this prayer :

O God of truth and Father of mercies, we thank you, because you have honoured our nature more than you did the holy patriarchs, who simply knew you as their God, whereas to us you have called yourself Father; and we now implore you, O Lord, to grant that the gifts of this new, honourable and glorious title may thrive more brightly in your Church as time passes by.

Deacon :   Father, give the blessing.

Priest :   Grant that we may, as children, call upon you, O heavenly Father, saying:

The Lord's Prayer is now recited, during which the altar is incensed by the deacon. The priest recites the Lord's Prayer in a low voice, and then says the following prayer in a low voice :

Lord of lords, God of gods, eternal King, Creator of everything, the Father of our Lord Jesus Christ, do not allow us to be tempted beyond our strength, but deliver us from evil and save us from disasters.

Deacon :   Father, give the blessing.

Priest :   For yours is the kingdom, the power and the glory, forever and ever. Amen.

A sermon may be preached at this point.

Priest :   Peace ✠ be with you all.

Choir :   And with you.

Deacon :   Let us adore God.

Choir :   In your presence, O Lord.

The priest then bows his head, and the people either kneel or bow very low, while the priest says the following prayer in a low voice :

> O Holy Spirit, you who are the life-giver and the giver of every good thing, have mercy upon these your people, who bowing before you, worship your divinity. Keep them free from sin and imprint on their souls the humility which their bodies assume, so that they may inherit and receive those things which are to come.

Deacon :   Father, give the blessing.

Priest :   Through Jesus Christ our Lord, to whom with you, O Holy Spirit and the Father Almighty, belong glory, dominion and honour, now and forevermore, worlds unceasing. Amen.

The altar is kissed three times. The ceremony of the Elevation is accompanied by the presence of tapers and the waving of fans by the attendant clergy. All present should kneel. The following exclamation is made by the deacon, who censes the altar, as the priest takes the bread in his hands and elevates it :

> Let us attend.

Priest :   Holy things to the holy *(he makes the elevation)*.

Choir :   One only is holy, even the Lord Jesus Christ, to the honour and glory of God the Father. Amen.

Deacon :   Father, give the blessing.

Priest :   Blessed be the holy Father, the true God.

Choir :   Amen.

Deacon :   Blessed be the Holy Spirit, the true God.

Choir :   Amen.

Deacon :   Father, give the blessing.

Priest :   Blessing and glory be to the Father, the Son and the Holy Spirit, now and forevermore, worlds unceasing.

The bread is replaced upon the altar, and the chalice is elevated. While the priest continues as below, the choir sings the following :

> Amen. The Father is holy; the Son is holy; the Spirit is holy. Blessing be, to the Father and to the Son and to the Holy Spirit, now and forevermore, worlds unceasing. Amen.

The priest bowing low, says the following prayer in a low voice :

> From your glorious heavenly throne, look down, O Lord Jesus Christ, and come and sanctify us; you who sit with your Father in heaven and who are sacrificed here, grant that you will give us your pure body and precious blood, so that we may give them to all your people.

The priest sets the chalice upon the altar, and removes the veil from it, after having kissed both the altar and the chalice. He then takes the bread and intincts it entirely with the contents of the chalice, while saying in a low voice :

> O Lord our God, who has called us Christians after the name of your only Son, and who has regenerated us through baptism, a spiritual cleansing for the remission of sins, and allowed us to become partakers of the most holy body and blood of your only Son, we now beg you, O Lord, to receive this holy Mystery in remission of our sins. We give thanks and glory to you, with the Son and the Holy Spirit, now and forevermore. Amen.

Deacon :   Father, give the blessing.

The priest now turns to face the people and elevates the bread, which he holds in his right hand. Holding the chalice in his left hand, he makes the sign of the cross with it over the people, saying in a loud voice :

> In holiness let us consume the ✠ holy and ✠ pure body and blood of our Lord and Saviour Jesus Christ, who, having descended from heaven, is distributed among us. He is the life ✠, the hope, the resurrection, the cleansing and the remission of sins. Sing a psalm to the Lord our God, the immortal and heavenly King, who sits among the cherubim.

The little curtain is now drawn, while the Fraction and Commixture takes place, the prayers of which appear below. Meanwhile the deacon continues :

> Sing a psalm to the Lord our God, all you choirs; sweetly sing spiritual songs. Because psalms, alleluias and spiritual songs are suited to him. O you his ministers, sing psalms and praise the Lord of lords.

During the singing of the hymns which appear below, the priest takes the bread in his hands, kisses it and says in a low voice the Confession of Faith :

> What blessing or thanks can we offer for this bread and cup?

But you only do we bless together with the Father and the
Holy Spirit, now and forevermore. Amen.

The priest, in a loud voice :

I confess and believe that you are the Christ, the Son of
God, who take away the sins of the world.

*The bread is then broken into three parts (some liturgists claim that it is
broken into four parts). The priest then puts one part into the chalice, while
saying :*

The fullness of the Holy Spirit.

*Then taking the other particles in his hand, he continues to pray in a low
voice, while holding the particles over the chalice :*

Holy Father, who called us by the same name as your only
Son and cleansed us by the baptism of spiritual washing,
allow us to receive of you holy Mysteries, for the forgiveness
of our sins. Imprint on us the grace of the Holy Spirit as you
did for the holy apostles who, when they had received him,
became the purifiers of the world. Now, O Lord and good
Father, remove the shadow of my sins and may we by our
participation in this become with his disciples partakers of
his Last Supper.

Disregard our unworthiness and do not remove from us
the grace of your Holy Spirit, but through your immeasurable love grant that this may purify us and remit our sins, as
our Lord Jesus Christ promised when he said: 'Whoever eats
my body and drinks my blood will live forever.' May this
cleanse us, then, who eat and drink of it, so that we may praise
the Father, the Son and the Holy Spirit, now and forevermore. Amen.

*While the priest has been saying the preceding prayer, the choir sings one of
the following hymns, which vary according to the day of the week :*

(Sunday) Christ is distributed and sacrificed. Alleluia. He
gives us his body as our food and redeems us with his holy
blood. Alleluia.
Come and approach near the Lord. Alleluia.
Taste and see how good the Lord is. Alleluia.
Bless the Lord in the heavens. Alleluia.
Bless him, all you angels of his. Alleluia.
Bless him, all you powers of his. Alleluia.

(Monday) O you, the true light and glory of the Father, O
you who are truly the reflection and image of his glory, you
the incarnate Word who established your holy Church on
an immovable foundation, O you who are truly the victim
being led to sacrifice, allow us to replenish ourselves at the
table of your wisdom. Have mercy upon us.

(Tuesday) O you, the Bread of Life, the food of immortality, the holy, ineffable and incomprehensible sacrament, you who descended from heaven to give man a new and better life, grant us, who thirst after you, the benefit of your tender mercy and have pity on us.

(Wednesday) O you who are both the door of heaven and the road to paradise, the Lord of life, before whom the angels and archangels sing hymns of praise, you who gave the apostles your pure body and blood, purify us so that we may be partakers of this divine sacrament, and be merciful to us.

(Thursday) O Word of the Father and great High Priest, you who are praised by the angels in heaven, you who suffered on the Cross for us and shed your blood for the salvation of the world, grant that our sins may be cleansed by the precious blood which you shed for our salvation, and may we see your mercy.

(Friday) O Lord Jesus Christ, the true and chief Cornerstone, who are praised by the angels in heaven and who shed your precious blood on the Cross for the eradication of the sins of the world, grant that we who depend upon you may drink from your chalice of salvation; have mercy upon us.

(Saturday) O Lamb of God, who are always sacrificed yet ever living, you who are worshipped by the heavenly armies, you who though free from sin were put to death and were sacrificed so as to reconcile us with the Father, purify us from sin and cleanse the souls of our faithful departed, and have mercy upon us.

Priest :   Peace ✠ be to you all.

I thank you, O Christ my King, who allow me, unworthy as I am, to receive your holy body and blood. Now I beg you, O Lord, that it will not condemn me, but will purify and remit my sins, and serve to heal both my soul and body, and so enable me to do good. Grant also that it may sanctify both my body and soul, and make me a suitable place for the most holy Trinity, so that together with the saints I may be considered worthy to praise you, with the Father and the Holy Spirit, now and forevermore. Amen.

THE PRAYER OF ST JOHN CHRYSOSTOM

I thank, exalt and praise you, O Lord my God, because today you have allowed me, unworthy as I am, to receive of the divine and awesome Mysteries of your most pure body and blood. Having this for my defence, I implore you that I might be kept in your sanctity, so that by remembering your goodness and kindness, I may live with you; because you, O Lord my God, endured the suffering and death on the Cross and rose from the dead for our sake.

Do not permit the enemy to hurt my soul, which has been sealed with the sign of your precious blood. O Lord God, erase from me all the stains of mortal sin, because you alone are sinless.

O Lord God, protect me from all disasters, drive away all my enemies and those who would wrong me. Direct my thoughts, words and deeds and be always with me, as you promised: 'He who eats my body and drinks my blood lives in me and I in him.' O Lover of mankind, you have said this; confirm these words which are your inviolable statements, because you, O God, are full of mercy, beneficence and the love of mankind. You have given us everything that is good, and to you belongs the glory with the Father and the Holy Spirit, now and forevermore, worlds unceasing. Amen.

The priest then blesses himself and says while holding a particle :

✠ I believe in the most holy Trinity, Father, Son and Holy Spirit.

The priest then consumes the particle, saying :

O Lord Jesus Christ, confidently I have received your holy body for the remission of my sins.

The priest then takes the chalice and consumes its contents, saying :

✠ O Lord Jesus Christ, confidently I have received your purifying blood.

The priest then makes the sign of the cross over his mouth, saying :

May your most pure body be for me ✠ a source of life and ✠ your precious blood cleanse and remit my sins.

The remainder of the host in the chalice is divided into smaller pieces. If a bishop is present, he communicates himself without a spoon; he simply dips his fingers into the chalice and removes a particle; he then breaks this particle into smaller pieces. During a bishop's communion, the curtain is drawn aside, and after he has blessed the people the curtain may be drawn, so that the other clergy may communicate. Following the deacon's communion, the people may approach and stand in front of the sanctuary. They are communicated from the chalice with intincted bread. The deacon, holding the chalice, says in a loud voice :

In the fear of God, approach with faith and communicate with awe.

Choir :   Our God, the Lord has appeared to us. He is blessed who comes in the name of the Lord.

The words of administration are :

> The body and blood of our Lord and Saviour Jesus Christ
> be to you for salvation and for a guide to eternal life.

If there is a priest among the communicants, he is given the chalice, so that he might communicate himself. If a deacon is present, he may receive the particle in the palm of the hands. The laity, kneeling, are communicated with the intincted bread and their lips are wiped with a towel which is held by the deacon. When the Communion is finished, the priest blesses the congregation either with his hand or with the sacred species, saying in a loud voice :

> O Lord save ✠ your people and bless your heritage;
> govern and exalt them now and forevermore. Amen.

The curtain is closed again, and the celebrant if a bishop resumes his mitre and emiphoron discarded earlier; whereas if the celebrant is a priest, he performs the ablutions, having consumed what is left in the chalice. The ablutions are performed at the altar. The minister who brings the wine and water kisses the altar when he presents them and when he retires. Water is taken only at the second ablution, unlike the Western custom. The choir meanwhile sings the following :

> O Lord, we have been filled with grace and have tasted your
> body and blood. May heavenly praise be given to the
> providence which always feeds us. Send us your spiritual
> blessing and may heavenly praise be given to him who
> always provides for us.

The priest resumes his saghavart and recites the following prayer secretly :

> We thank you, O Father almighty, who prepared a shelter
> for us, the holy Church, the temple of holiness, where the
> holy Trinity is glorified. Alleluia.
>
> We thank you, O Christ our King, who by the life-creating
> and holy body and blood have given life to us. Mercifully
> grant us salvation. Alleluia.
>
> O Spirit of truth we thank you for having founded your
> Church. Keep it pure in the faith of the most holy Trinity,
> now and forevermore. Amen.

Meanwhile the deacon says :

> May we who have received these divine, holy, heavenly,
> eternal and most pure, incorruptible Mysteries in faith,
> continually pray peacefully to the Lord. Let us thank him for
> all that he has given us.

Choir :   O Lord, we thank you for having fed us from your immortal
> table. You have given your body and blood for the salvation
> of the world and as life for our souls.

While the choir sings this hymn, the priest recites in a low voice the Prayer of Thanksgiving :

> O Christ our God, we thank you, who out of your goodness has given us the food necessary for the sanctification of our lives. Keep us holy and blameless under your divine protection and nourish us in the gardens of your holy and good pleasure, so that being fortified against all the efforts of the devil we may be thought worthy to hear your holy command to follow you, the one victorious and true shepherd, and to take the place prepared for us in the kingdom of heaven.
>
> For you, O our Lord God and Saviour Jesus Christ, are blessed with the Father and the Holy Spirit, now and forevermore, worlds unceasing. Amen.
>
> Peace ✚ be with all.
>
> To the inscrutable, incomprehensible divinity of the holy, consubstantial, life-giving and undivided Trinity, belong glory, dominion and honour, now and forevermore, worlds unceasing. Amen.

At its conclusion, the deacon says :

> Father, give the blessing.

The curtain is opened and the celebrant takes up the Book of Gospels, kisses the altar and then comes to the centre of the choir, accompanied by the deacons. Turning then towards the altar, he says aloud :

> O Lord, bless those who bless you, and make those holy who trust you; save your people, bless your heritage and protect the fullness of your Church. Sanctify those who love the splendour of your house; may they be imbued with your divine power. Do not abandon us who trust you. Give peace to all your churches, to your priests, to all Christian kings and their armed defence forces, and to your people everywhere, because every good and perfect gift is from you in heaven, the Father of Light, and to you be glory, dominion, honour and worship now and forevermore, worlds unceasing. Amen.

Choir :   Blessed is the name of the Lord, now and forevermore *(this is said three times)*.

The priest then turns towards the people and says :

> O Christ our God, who has completed all that was promised in the Law and the Prophets; you are our Redeemer, you have perfectly obeyed the Father; fill us with your Holy Spirit.

Deacon :   Stand up *(Orthi)*.

The priest blesses the people with the Book of Gospels :

>   Peace ✠ be with all.

Choir :   And with you.

Deacon :   Listen attentively.

Priest :   The holy Gospel according to St John.

Choir :   Glory be to you, O Lord our God.

Deacon :   Let us be attentive *(Proschumen)*.

Choir :   God speaks.

The priest removes the saghavart for the Last Gospel, which he reads facing the people. The extract from the Gospel is taken usually from John 1 : 1–18, except from Easter Eve until Pentecost Eve, when the extract is taken from John 21 : 15–19. If a bishop has been the celebrant, he reads the Gospel facing the people, accompanied by clerics holding tapers and a deacon holding a censer. At the conclusion of the Gospel, the priest resumes his saghavart and the choir sings :

>   Glory to you, O Lord God.

Deacon :   O Lord, by the holy Cross and the Gospel, we implore you to deliver us from our sins and may we be saved by the grace of your mercy. Lord, have mercy upon us *(this is said three times)*.

Priest :   O Christ our God, keep your servants under the shadow of your holy and most honoured Cross; deliver us from both visible and invisible enemies, and grant that we may thank and praise you, together with the Father and the Holy Spirit, now and forevermore, worlds unceasing.

The fans are shaken during the singing of the next versicle by the choir :

>   I will bless the Lord always; his praise will always be in my mouth.

Turning towards the people, who are being incensed by the deacon, the priest blesses them three times saying :

>   May you be blessed ✠ through the grace of the Holy Spirit. Go in peace, and may the Lord always be with you. Amen.

The Dissident Armenians say the following :

>   ✠ May the Holy Spirit remain with you and the power from heaven protect you.

The Eulogia or distribution of the blessed bread at the conclusion of the liturgy is accompanied by the choir singing Psalm 34, followed by the Gloria.

The priest finally turns towards the east and bowing three times towards the altar says :

> O Lord Jesus Christ, have mercy upon me.

The priest then enters the sacristy, where he unvests and comes before the altar ; he bows three times and leaves.

The Coptic Liturgy

INTRODUCTION

The Coptic liturgy was deeply influenced by monastic elements and like a monastic liturgy it is very lengthy and slow in movement. It is a liturgy in which the hymns and chants are varied at random, the metre of which is interspersed with clashing cymbals.

The semi-isolation of origin and history has had a marked effect on Christian Egypt. From the time of St Athanasius, the early patriarchs of Alexandria relied very heavily on the support of the Egyptian monks. Under St Cyril not only was the monastic influence very apparent but the Syrian influence also made itself felt; consequently all the doctrinal and liturgical development that occurred in Syria was transmitted to Egypt. To the present day, following the reforms of the twelfth to fifteenth century, Syrian forms are still employed in the administration of the sacraments, and many hymns of the Office, particularly the 'Theotokial' (in honour of our Lady), are Syrian.

1. History

According to tradition the church of Alexandria was founded by St Mark the Evangelist. Initially the successors of St Mark were the only metropolitans and they exercised jurisdiction over a very large area. As time went by, more metropolitan sees were established and the metropolitan at Alexandria became known as the arch-metropolitan. The use of the title 'patriarch' did not come into use until the fifth century.

Until the second Ecumenical Council the bishop of Alexandria ranked second to the bishop of Rome. This position was subsequently claimed by the patriarch of Constantinople, but neither Rome nor Alexandria recognized this claim for many years.

Eusebius provides us with a list of the early arch-metropolitans until the time of Julian (†189). It was Julian's successor Demetrius who deposed and excommunicated Origen. Of the ante-Nicene bishops who ruled the church so illustriously, Dionysius and Alexander should be mentioned, as also St Athanasius and St Cyril. St Athanasius (†373) was supported by Rome and was one of the principal opponents of Arianism. Between the death of St Athanasius and the succession of St Cyril, Peter II was in charge but was forced to seek refuge in Rome to avoid persecution by the Arians. The renown and power of the patriarchate of Alexandria reached its peak under St Cyril. The decline of this office dates from about the middle of the fifth century.

It was under Dioscorus, St Cyril's successor, that the church became most involved in the Monophysite heresy. After some six years of controversy Dioscorus was deposed and his teaching condemned by the Council of Chalcedon (451). With the election of his successor Proterius, schism followed.

The schism was clearly divided between the Catholics or Orthodox and the Monophysites. The Catholics maintained faith in the two natures of Christ, as determined by the Council of Chalcedon, while the Monophysites followed the teaching of Dioscorus, which alleged that in the one person of the incarnate Christ there was only a single divine nature and not a twofold nature, human and divine. The Orthodox Catholics became known as Melchites or Royalists, while the dissidents were known as Jacobites. The see of Alexandria was alternately occupied by these rival parties and each communion maintained a separate and independent succession. This bifurcation was firmly established in 567.

During the Saracen invasion, the Jacobites, urged on by their animosity towards the Melchites, gave up their cities to the invaders, which gave the Jacobites an ascendency over the Melchites and an influence which they earnestly desired. Until then the Melchites, aided by the emperor, had wielded immense civil power, and the loss of this power was accompanied by a corresponding loss of many churches and monasteries. After Patriarch Peter died in 654 the Melchite succession was broken and remained so for many years. Ironically the Jacobites along with the Melchites suffered badly as a result of renewed Saracen persecution. When the patriarchate was restored under Cosmas in 727 the church was in a deplorable state due to indolence and ignorance.

The Jacobites found themselves in no better position. They were constantly beleagured by internal disputes, not the least of which concerned auricular confession and this controversy between the Jacobite patriarchs of Alexandria and Antioch eventually severed the friendly relations that had existed between them.

For many years the Jacobites were without a patriarch and, despite appeals to the pope for assistance, both they and the Melchites suffered appallingly up to the persecutions of the fourteenth century. During this dark period, the Melchites came under the influence of the Byzantine patriarch and became involved in the confusion that accompanied the Greek Schism.

We will now briefly trace the historical development of these two branches of the Coptic Church under two headings, Monophysite and Catholic.

1) *Monophysite*—Europe became very conscious of Egypt and in the

wake of its interest came Protestant missionaries. The arrival of European influence in Egypt brought peace to the Copts. It has been suggested that the iconoclasm of Cyril IV was attributable to the Protestant influence. European investment and wealth brought with it many problems, however, and gave rise to internal disputes among the Christians of the country.

The lack of central church organization provoked the erection of a council of lay people to undertake the administrative work of the patriarchate. The principal complaint of the lay reform body was that concerning the administration of church revenues and the election of candidates for ordination to the priesthood.

Patriarch Cyril V Makar would not surrender his 'rights' and his obstinancy forced the Khedive Abbas Hilmi to require him to retire to a monastery. This caused such an outburst of indignation that the patriarch was recalled. His death in 1927 proved to be a turning-point in the disagreement between the bishops and the reformers: the whole problem was presented to the government for adjudication and it was the government's recommendation that a council, the Maglis Milli, should be set up to administer the church's temporal affairs.

This council was established in 1927, but it is sad to relate that it did nothing to abate the frequent eruptions of difference that occurred between the bishops and the laity.

2) *Catholic*—The establishment of a Franciscan mission in the seventeenth century did little to effect reunion and despite the efforts of Fr Agathangelo (of Vendome) it was the behaviour of the resident European Catholics in the country that proved to be the great stumbling-block.

In the late seventeenth century the Jesuits came to Cairo, but again very little was achieved. The conversion of the dissident Amba Athanasius was a stimulus to progress, and Coptic liturgical texts began to be printed in Rome. But despite the good intentions of Athanasius, he lacked sufficient conviction and returned to Monophysitism.

About forty years elapsed before a new vicar apostolic could be consecrated. Maximos Joed, who had been nominated in 1824, was consecrated by the Melkite patriarch of Antioch.

Because of many difficulties, both jurisdictional and organizational, Pope Leo XII decided to erect a patriarchate for the Catholic Copts, but his proposal remained unfulfilled for many years. Pope Leo XIII finally appointed Cyril Makarios as administrator of the Catholic Copts, and in 1899 Makarios became patriarch. However, his position became quite untenable and after a short-lived administration he resigned. It was not until Abba Mark II Khuzam was appointed that—promoted by his energetic and tireless efforts—the long-awaited and effective apostolate was firmly established and progress became apparent.

Iconostase of St Anthony the
Great, Coptic Catholic
Cathedral, Cairo

Cardinal Stephanos Sidarousse,
Patriarch of Alexandria
(Catholic Coptic)

II. *Church buildings*

A Coptic church is divided for the whole of its length into the sanctuary, choir, nave and narthex. While both sexes may mingle on the south side of the nave, the north side is reserved exclusively for women.

Between the sanctuary and choir, there is the iconostasis. Within the sanctuary (*haikal*) there are three altars in a line, standing clear of the wall; these altars are usually made of stone covered with wood and the whole structure is covered with silken cloths, upon which stand two or more candles.

III. *Vestments*

The vestments used in the Coptic Church are similar to those worn in the Byzantine rite. However, there is a difference in that the chasuble or *Burnus* is open down the front, rather similar to the Syrian *phelonion* and quite like a Western cope.

Bishops may wear the *omophorion*, which is a vestment of great antiquity and corresponds to the Western pallium, except that it is very much longer. It is made of wool and is said to represent the lost sheep of human nature being carried on the shoulders of the 'shepherd of the flock'. Occasionally the Coptic bishops may wear the *sakkos*, which is rather like an elaborate dalmatic; it is a loose-fitting vestment with long sleeves and is usually heavily embroidered; in the West it is worn by the deacon over the alb and cassock during a solemn celebration of the liturgy.

The *tailasan* is worn by dissident priests and consists of a broad strip of embroidered material ending in a hood. Its Western equivalent is probably the amice. In small and very poor churches the liturgy is sometimes celebrated by a priest wearing only the alb and tailasan.

While dissident priests wear a turban out-of-doors, the Catholic clergy wear a cylindrical black hat over which bishops wear a veil.

An odd feature of the Coptic rite is that the celebrant must be barefooted during the celebration of the eucharistic liturgy.

IV. *Altar vessels*

The vessels of the Coptic rite are the same as those used in the Byzantine rite with a few minor differences; for example, the *diskos* or paten is larger and deeper. Among the Dissidents, the lance is not used in the preparation of the bread. The *kurbana* or bread is leavened and usually very thick.

V. *Liturgical books and language*

The books needed for the celebration of the eucharistic liturgy are the Khulaji (priest's book) and the Kutmarus (a lectionary containing lessons from the Holy Scriptures) as well as the Synaxar (roughly equivalent to the Western Martyrology). The Synaxar is sometimes read instead of the Acts of the Apostles. Another book is called the Book of the Ministry of the Deacons; it contains the Diakonika, the responses together with the variable and fixed hymns.

Both Coptic and Ethiopic Uniats have books especially prepared for them, which differ only to the extent that the name 'Monophysite' has been omitted and that of Chalcedon substituted in the Commemorations. The 'Filioque' is of course added to the Creed.

The name 'Copt' was applied to the Egyptians by the Arabs. Initially it served to identify the non-hellenized populace of the country. Finally 'Coptic' was used for their language and applied to their liturgical rite. Coptic was the written language spoken by the Egyptians from about the third until the tenth century. The language was largely supplanted by Arabic but in a few places it appears to have survived until the close of the seventeenth century. In essence it was the language of ancient Egypt into which many Greek words became incorporated and the whole is written in an alphabet closely resembling the Greek alphabet.

VI.   *Sacraments*

1) *Baptism*—Among the Copts the administration of baptism is a very long ceremony involving blessings, prayers, anointing with holy oil, and the consecration of the water with a series of Lessons and a Gospel.

During the rite, the Coptic catechumen explicitly declares his faithfulness to Christ, rather significantly unlike the Syrian renouncement by way of interrogation.

An interesting feature of the Coptic rite, like that of the Chaldeans, is that it is fashioned after the eucharistic liturgy, where the consecration of the water replaces the Anaphora.

The child to be baptized is immersed in water three times by the priest, who says: 'N. I baptize you in the Name of the Father . . .' Under the most necessitous circumstances, baptism can be administered simply by the pouring of water. Monophysite Copts however do not recognize the validity of lay baptism.

Circumcision must be given before baptism, and this is attributed to Cyril III (1235–43). But circumcision has now lost its religious significance. Some Judaic food restrictions are also observed by the Copts.

2) *Confirmation*—This sacrament immediately follows baptism. The person to be confirmed is anointed with thirty-six anointings, each being administered with a different formula, followed by the imposition of hands and a breathing on the child or adult with the words: 'Be blessed with the blessing of heaven's angels. May our Lord Jesus Christ

bless you. Receive the Holy Spirit; be clean vessels through our Lord
Jesus Christ, to whom be glory with his Father and the Holy Spirit
forevermore.'

3) *Penance*—Among the Copts, the practice varies immensely. The
most common form is referred to as confessing 'to the thurible'; this
refers to the custom of recalling one's sins during the first censing of the
liturgy, as this censing is considered to be purificatory and is followed
by the Prayer of Absolution. Apart from this practice, auricular confession is quite a protracted affair and falls into three divisions: in the
first part, the penitent seeks Christ's forgiveness; in the second part,
the penitent requests forgiveness from the Holy Trinity through the
Church; finally the penitent says: 'I have sinned; absolve me', to which
the priest replies, 'God absolve you'.

Monophysite bishops, priests and deacons are not required to
confess their sins, while the lay people do so quite rarely and then only
after a very general and vague declaration of offences.

4) *Eucharist*—The Eucharist is received by the Copts under both
species, either separately or by intinction. The words of ministration
are: 'This is indeed the body and blood of Emmanuel, our God', to
which the recipient should reply 'Amen'. Among the Monophysites,
the reception of the Eucharist is quite infrequent.

5) *Holy orders*—The ordination of a reader usually involves simply
a prayer and blessing; that of subdeacon requires the imposition of
hands on the temples. An ordinand for the diaconate is signed on the
forehead with the sign of the cross and the right hand of the bishop is
imposed while the formula is recited. The deacon is subsequently in-
vested with the stole. The same applies for priestly ordinations, except
that the prayer is as follows: 'Fill him with the Holy Spirit and the
grace . . . We call you N. to be a priest for the ministry of the altar
which was first given to right believers, in the Name of the Father and
of the Son and of the Holy Spirit. Amen.'

Episcopal consecration consists of a profession of faith, prayers and
the following proclamation which is read by the archdeacon: 'Divine
Grace, which gives strength to weakness and supplies what is lacking,
chooses N. as bishop. Let us then pray for him that the grace of the
Holy Spirit may come upon him.' The universal use of this prayer in
the East since about the fourth century is most impressive and interesting. During the consecration of the bishop, the consecrator's right hand
is placed on the consecrand's head and the co-consecrators place their
hands on the bishop-elect's shoulders and arms.

A short Epiclesis follows the prayer given above; then, after the
laying on of hands, the pastoral staff is delivered and finally the Book
of Gospels is placed on the new bishop's breast.

6) *Marriage*—The administration of this sacrament is composed of

two parts, the betrothal and the crowning. The betrothal consists of
the reading of the Epistle (Ephes 5:22–6:3) and the Gospel (Mt
19:1–6), prayers, the Creed and Thanksgiving, as well as an unusual
feature of Coptic weddings, the blessing of the bride's dowry of clothing
and jewellery. The crowning is accompanied by the anointing of the
bride and bridegroom's hands and wrists, followed by the crowning of
both. The ceremony is drawn to a colourful close with the singing of
appropriate hymns and antiphons.

7) *Anointing or the office of the lamp*—Like most Coptic sacraments,
this one is rather lengthy and involves the lighting of seven lamps,
accompanied by the recitation of the appropriate Lessons, Psalms,
Gospels and prayers, all recited by seven priests. At the conclusion of
the foregoing, the Book of Gospels is laid on the sick person's head,
while the throat, wrists and forehead are anointed. Today it is more
usual to have only one priest in attendance, who administers the
sacrament alone.

Among the Monophysites, the sacrament is given not only to the
sick but to the healthy as well, as it is considered to act both as a
prophylactic against illnesses as well as to effect absolution.

VII.   *Clergy*

The Catholic patriarch is known as the 'Patriarch of Alexandria and of
All the Preaching of St Mark'. Unlike his brother patriarch, the
Catholic patriarch is nominated by Rome and is not elected by his
fellow bishops. The full title of the dissident patriarch is 'The Most
Holy Father and Patriarch of the Great City of Alexandria and of All
Egypt, of the City of Our God, Jerusalem, and of the Pentapolis of
Libya, Nubia, Ethiopia, Africa and of All the Places where St Mark
preached'. He is elected by his fellow bishops and clergy, who additionally consult the laity. The dissident Coptic patriarch ordains all
bishops himself and alone consecrates the chrism which is distributed
throughout all the dioceses. In government the patriarch is assisted by
a religious council.

Among the Dissidents there are a multitude of sees, and when one
becomes vacant, a monk is chosen by an election carried out among the
clergy and laity. This monk, on becoming a bishop, must, like all other
Coptic bishops, be at least fifty years old and is bound to perpetual
abstinence from fish and meat. By way of contrast with their dissident
brethren, the number of Catholic Coptic sees is very small indeed.
When a see becomes vacant, it is filled by a priest nominated by the
patriarch and synod.

VIII.   *Calendar*

The Copts date their first years from the Diocletian accession in 284.

The Catholics of Lower Egypt calculate Easter by the Gregorian method, while those of Upper Egypt employ the Julian computation.

During any ecclesiastical year, there are five principal fasts: the pre-Lenten fast of Nineveh, lasting three days; the Great Fast of Lent, lasting fifty-five days; the fast before the Nativity, lasting twenty-eight days; the fast of the Apostles, which occurs after the Ascension; and the fast of the Virgin, which is commemorated before the Assumption.

IX.   *Conclusion*

As would be expected, the Catholic Copt has acquired many Western customs, e.g. he blesses himself from left to right and genuflects, as against the customary prostration on both knees. Benediction of the Blessed Sacrament, the rosary and other Western devotions are becoming increasingly common, but in Upper Egypt the influence of the West is not so apparent.

Although the Dissident Copts officially reaffirm their Monophysite faith, one is left with the impression that the subtely of it has certainly evaded the bulk of the faithful. The Dissidents, unlike their Catholic brethren, do not use a cross upon the altar.

X.   *Sources of liturgical texts*

Brightman, F. E., *Liturgies Eastern and Western,* Oxford, 1896.
Bute, Marquis of, *The Coptic Morning Service for the Lord's Day,* London, 1906.
Butler, A. J., *Ancient Coptic Churches of the East,* 2 volumes, Oxford, 1884.
Malan, S. C., *Original Documents of the Coptic Church,* London, 1875.
Petit Paroissien des Liturgies Orientales, Libya, 1941.
Renaudot, E., *Liturgiarum Orientalium Collectio,* Paris, 1716.
Tuki, R., *Missale Coptice et Arabia,* Rome, 1736.

COPTIC LITURGY

It is customary for the Office of the Morning Incense to be read, but in its absence, the following procedure is adopted. The priest goes to the altar, bearing the chalice and paten; placing them upon the altar, he kisses it, and then blesses himself saying :

In the Name of the Father and of the Son and of the Holy Spirit, one God. Amen.

The priest turns halfway around, facing towards the people, and blesses them saying :

Have mercy upon us.

Choir :   O God, Father, almighty and all-holy Trinity, have mercy upon us. O Lord God of powers, be with us. Truly without your aid, we are helpless in our difficulties.

All :   Our Father . . .

The priest silently says the Prayer of Preparation of the Altar :

O Lord, you who know us all and our inmost thoughts, who are so holy and live among the saints, who are sinless and readily forgive sin; you, O Lord, who know my unworthiness and unsuitability to presume to approach these Mysteries, grant me, a sinner, mercy and forgiveness, so that I might find the grace and strength that come from heaven *(the priest unveils the chalice and lays it on the altar, together with the paten and spoon; the spoon was once used by the Catholics, but is no longer)*, so that I might commence and be made suitable to perform the liturgy according to your pleasure and will, as a sweet, fragrant incense.

Be among us, O Lord, and bless us, for you are the forgiver of our sins, the illuminary of our souls, our life, our strength and our confidence. To you, O Lord, we offer praise, glory and worship, the Father, Son and Holy Spirit, now and forever, worlds unceasing. Amen.

O Lord, you have taught us this great mystery of salvation; you have called us, even though we are unworthy, to be your ministers at the altar. O Lord, make us worthy, by the operation of the Holy Spirit, to complete this service, so that without meriting condemnation we may offer a sacrifice of praise and glory. O God, the dispenser of grace and our Saviour, grant that our sacrifice may be accepted

by you, for my sins and for the sins of your people, for this
sacrifice is holy, according to the gift of the Holy Spirit, in
Jesus Christ, our Lord, to whom with you and the Holy
Spirit, the life-giver, all glory, honour and worship are due,
now and ever, worlds unceasing. Amen.

*The priest kisses the altar and turns to the west, choosing the bread presented
to him by the deacon; the bread is kissed and then laid upon the altar; then
the wine is examined and the priest washes his hands:*

With the pure in heart, I will wash my hands clean and take
my place among them at the altar, Lord, listening there to
the sound of your praises.

*The priest may continue the rest of Psalm 25 if he chooses. Following the
Lavabo, the priest partly dries his hands, and then rubs the bread saying:*

O Lord, grant that our Sacrifice may be acceptable, for my
sins and for the sins of your people, and may it be consecrated
by the gift of the Holy Spirit in Jesus Christ our Lord,
through whom and with whom, together with the Holy
Spirit, the life-giver of one substance with you, be all glory,
honour and worship given, now and ever, worlds unceasing.
Amen.

*The celebrant now directs his intention for the liturgy of the day, whether
for the living or for the dead, etc. The petitions usually take a very short
form. Following the recital, the priest takes the bread in his hand in a silk
veil and walks around the altar, preceded by a deacon carrying the wine, and
another deacon bearing a taper. During this procession, the choir sings as
follows:*

Alleluia. Man's mind will praise you, and will rejoice in
your presence. Alleluia. The sacrifices and offerings are
presented to you. Alleluia.

During the Paschal festival, the following is sung:

Alleluia. This is the day that the Lord has designed; let us
be happy and glad of it. O Lord, save us and direct our
footsteps. He is blessed that comes in the name of the Lord.
Alleluia.

While the choir sings, the priest recites the following:

May glory and honour be given to the holy Trinity, the
Father, Son and Holy Spirit.
    Grant peace and holiness to the one, holy, catholic and
apostolic Church. Amen.
    O Lord, remember those who have brought their gifts to
you, and those who have had their gifts brought for them;
grant them all, O Lord, their reward. O Lord, be pleased

to remember those who have asked for prayers; may they be remembered in heaven.

By now the priest has usually completed the procession and is standing in front of the altar; he holds the bread in one hand close to the cruets of wine, held by the deacon. The priest blesses both the bread and wine, saying:

In the name of the Father, and of the Son, and of the Holy Spirit, one God.

The priest again blesses the offerings:

Blessed be ✠ God, the Father almighty. Amen.

Deacon: Amen.

Priest: Blessed be ✠ his only Son, our Lord Jesus Christ. Amen.

Deacon: Amen.

Priest: Blessed be ✠ the Holy Spirit, the Comforter. Amen.

Deacon: Amen.

The bread is then placed on the paten and the priest recites the following in silence:

Glory, honour and dominion to the all-holy Trinity, the Father, Son and Holy Spirit.

During the following prayer of the deacon, the priest says:

Grant, O Lord, that our sacrifice for my sins and the ignorance of your people be acceptable; may it be sanctified by the gift of the Holy Spirit, in Christ Jesus our Lord.

Wine is poured into the chalice, while the deacon says:

Amen. Amen. Amen. One holy Father, one holy Son and one Holy Spirit. Amen. Blessed be the Lord God forever. Amen. May all nations and people bless the Lord, because his mercy has been shown towards us, and may the truth of the Lord be demonstrated everywhere. Amen. Alleluia.

People: Glory be to the Father, and to the Son, and to the Holy Spirit, as it was in the beginning, is now, and shall always be forevermore. Amen. Alleluia.

The priest, turning west, blesses the congregation, saying:

Peace be with you all.

People: And with you.

Priest: Let us give thanks to the good and merciful Lord, the Father of our Lord and Saviour Jesus Christ, because he has protected, assisted and preserved us. He has redeemed us, spared us and has enabled us to be here at this moment. Let us all pray that the almighty Lord and God will preserve us in peace today and forevermore.

Deacon :   Let us pray.

People :   Lord, have mercy.

Priest :   O Lord God, the Father of our Lord and Saviour Jesus Christ, we give you thanks for everything, because you have protected, assisted and preserved us, because you have redeemed us, spared us and have enabled us to be here today.

Deacon :   Let us pray that God will have mercy upon us, will mercifully hear us and assist us, and, in receiving our prayers and requests from the saints on our behalf, will grant us the forgiveness of our sins, so that we will be made worthy to receive his holy and blessed Mysteries and so obtain the remission of our sins.

People :   Lord, have mercy.

The priest prays in silence :

Therefore we beg and pray, O Lover of mankind, that you will grant us the grace to pass this day and all the days of our life in peace and in your fear. All envy, temptation and wickedness *(the priest now blesses himself and continues)* take away *(he now makes the sign of the cross over his left shoulder)* from us *(he does the same over his right shoulder)* and from all your people *(he blesses similarly the altar)* and from this altar. But allow all such things as are suitable and useful for us. Because by your power you have enabled us to walk upon serpents and scorpions and the manifestations of the devil, do not permit us to be tempted beyond our endurance, but deliver us from evil through the gracious, merciful love towards mankind of your only Son, our Lord and Saviour Jesus Christ, through whom and with whom and the Holy Spirit, the life-giver, who is consubstantial with you, all glory, honour, power and worship are due, forevermore, until the end of the world. Amen.

The priest says the Prayer of Oblation in silence :

O Lord Jesus Christ, the only Son and Word of God the Father, consubstantial with him and with the Holy Spirit, you are the living bread which came down from heaven and presented itself as a spotless lamb for the salvation of the world. We pray and beg out of your goodness, O Lover of mankind *(the priest points towards the bread)*, to look favourably upon this bread *(he points also towards the chalice)* and this cup, which we have placed upon the holy table. *(He blesses both, saying:)* ✠ Bless them. ✠ Bless and transform them *(he points to the bread)* that this bread may become your body *(he points to the chalice)* and this mixture of water and wine which is in this cup may become your adorable blood, that it may become for us assistance and healing, physical and spiritual. For you are our God and to you, with your good Father and the Holy Spirit, the life-giver, consubstantial with you, are due glory and power forevermore. Amen.

The bread and wine are covered. After kneeling, the priest rises, kisses the altar and, together with the deacon, proceeds round it. They then proceed out of the sanctuary, in so doing they are required to put their left foot first. The priest then pronounces the prayer of Absolution silently over the kneeling congregation:

The Lord Jesus Christ, the only Son and Word of God the Father, who by his saving and life-giving sufferings broke all the bonds of sin; who breathed into the faces of his holy disciples and apostles, saying to them, 'Receive the Holy Spirit; whose sins you remit, they are remitted; and whose sins you retain they are retained'; you also, O Lord, by your holy apostles have given us your priests in your holy Church this same power of binding and loosing; we therefore beg your goodness, O Lover of mankind, for your servants, my fathers and brothers, who are now bowing their heads before your glory; grant them and us your mercy and release us from the bonds of our sins, if we have in any way sinned against you, knowingly or otherwise. O merciful God, you who love mankind and know our weaknesses, grant us the remission of our sins. *(The priest blesses himself:)* ✠ Bless us *(he blesses the sacred ministers)* ✠ purify and absolve us *(he blesses the people)* ✠ and absolve all your people. *(He calls to mind all those whose remembrance has been requested.)* Fearfully may we be led to do your holy and good will, for you are our God and to you, with your good Father and the Holy Spirit, the life-giver, who is consubstantial with you, are due all glory, honour and power forevermore. Amen.

During the prayer which follows, the priest makes the sign of the cross towards each person or group mentioned if present:

May your servants who serve you today—the abbot; the priest(s), my father(s); the priests and the deacon; the clergy and all the people and my own frailty—may they be absolved from their sins, by the authority of the all-holy Trinity, the Father, the Son and the Holy Spirit; by the authority of the holy, catholic and apostolic Church, the twelve Apostles, Mark the Ecstatic Apostle, Evangelist and Martyr, holy

Athanasius, John, Cyril, Gregory and Basil, together with the three hundred and eighteen at Nicaea, the hundred and fifty at Constantinople, and the two hundred at Ephesus, as well as the six hundred and thirty who were together at Chalcedon; also by the authority of the Holy Father Pope N., of our father, Archbishop Abba N., and his auxiliary Bishop Abba N., and by me. For your holy name is blessed and glorious, O Father, Son and Holy Spirit, forevermore. Amen.

Everybody rises. The priest enters the sanctuary, kissing the altar; he places incense in the censer. While he recites the Prayer of Incense, the choir sings the following anthems:

This is the pure golden censer, containing fragrant incense, held in the hands of Aaron the priest, who offers it upon your altar.

The golden censer is the Virgin, while the incense cloud is the Saviour. She has carried him who has saved us and forgives our sins.

You are the censer of pure gold, holding live coals of blessed fire.

The priest says the Prayer of Incense in a low voice:

The mighty and eternal God, who is without beginning and without end, who is omnipresent and mighty in all his works, be with us and remain with us all. Purify our bodies and sanctify our souls, so that we may be cleansed from every sin which we have committed voluntarily or involuntarily. May we be able to offer you reasonable offerings and sacrifices.

Deacon: Let us remember the sacrifice we are offering. Lord, have mercy *(the Monophysites do not add this last ejaculation).*

Priest: May they enter the holy of holies. And we pray you, O our Lord, to remember the peace of your one, holy, catholic and apostolic Church.

Deacon: Pray for the peace of the one, holy and apostolic Orthodox Church of God.

The priest, kissing the altar on its south side, continues:

Which is from one end of the world to the other. Remember O Lord, our patriarch, the holy father, the Pontiff Abba N.

Deacon: Pray for our pontiff, the Pope Abba N., Pope and Patriarch, and his fellow servant, the Bishop Abba N. Lord, have mercy.

The priest and deacon now proceed around the altar, kissing it at each corner. The priest prays :

> May he be preserved in safety for us for many years. O Lord, remember your faithful congregation of faithful and be pleased to bless them.

Deacon : Pray for this holy church and all our congregation.

The priest having returned to the front of the altar continues :

> Grant, O Lord, that we may retain possession of these churches, without any disturbance or hindrance, and that we may retain them according to your will, so that they may be houses of prayer, holiness and blessing.

The deacon now leaves the sanctuary, while the priest continues :

> Arise, O Lord God; may your enemies and all those who hate your holy name depart in haste.

The priest again processes around the altar. Having arrived at the east side, he says :

> And may your people be blessed many times over and may they always do your will; through the gracious mercy and love towards mankind that your only Son, our Lord and God, the Saviour Jesus Christ, has for us.

The priest goes around the altar a third time, saying :

> Through whom are due to you, with him and the Holy Spirit, the life-giver, consubstantial with you, glory, honour, power and worship, now and forevermore. Amen.

Having finished the circuit, the priest kisses the altar and leaves the sanctuary, while the choir sing a short anthem. This having been concluded, the priest censes the altar three times, saying the following :

> We adore You, O Christ, and your good Father and the Holy Spirit, because you have come and saved us.
> In the presence of the angels, I will sing praises before you and I will worship in your holy temple.
> As for me, I will now enter your house and will worship in your holy temple.

The icon or picture of the Blessed Virgin is censed three times, while the priest says the following :

> Hail Mary, the most beautiful dove, which carried the Word of God for us; we greet you with the Archangel Gabriel, saying: Hail, full of grace, the Lord is with you. Hail, O Virgin, the glory of our race; you have carried Emmanuel for us. We pray that you will remember us before our Lord Jesus Christ, that he will forgive our sins.

The other icons and pictures are censed and then the clergy are censed. The deacon then announces his intention to read the Lesson from St Paul:

> Paul, who was the servant of our Lord Jesus Christ, who was called to be an Apostle.

Facing east, he then reads the Lesson in Coptic, while the choir is censed by the priest, saying:

> May the blessings of Paul, the Apostle of Jesus Christ, be upon us. Amen.

The priest then proceeds through the church, censing the congregation and saying:

> Come, let us worship Jesus Christ, who is the same yesterday, today and forevermore.

The phrase 'Come, let us worship' is repeated many times by the Catholic Copts but is not used at all by the Monophysites. After incensing the congregation, the priest returns to the altar where he offers incense, saying the following in silence (Monophysites only):

> O God, who received the confession of the thief upon the Cross, be pleased to hear and receive the confession of your people, and forgive all their sins, for the sake of your holy name and according to your mercies and not because of our sins.

When the Lesson in Coptic is finished, the people say:

> May grace and peace be with you. Amen.

Facing west, the deacon reads the Lesson in Arabic, during which the priest recites in silence the Prayer of St Paul:

> O God of knowledge and wisdom, you reveal all things that are hidden and give the Word and his power to all those who preach the Gospel; of your goodness you called Paul who had been a persecutor and called him to become a chosen Apostle and preacher of the Gospel of Christ, our God; O God, Lover of mankind, we earnestly beg you to graciously grant us and all your people minds free from distractions and imbued with crystal-like lucidity, so that we might learn and appreciate your holy teachings which have come to us by him; and just as he was made in the same likeness of you, so may we be made like him in deed and firmness of doctrine, so that we may praise your holy name and glory in your Cross. You are he to whom we offer praise, glory and worship; the Father, the Son and the Holy Spirit, now and forevermore. Amen.

The Lesson is now read from the Catholic Epistles, before which the reader says:

The Lesson from the Epistle of N., my beloved brethren.

At its conclusion, the people answer:

Do not love the world, nor the things that are in it. The world and its attractions pass away, but he who does the will of God will live forever. Amen.

The Epistle is then read in Arabic, during which the priest recites the Prayer of the Catholic Epistle:

O Lord God, who revealed the mystery of Christ's Gospel through your holy Apostles, according to the power of your grace that empowered them to go through the world and proclaim the good news of your mercy, may we be made worthy to share with them. May we always walk in their paths and imitate them in their struggles. Preserve your holy Church, which you founded through them; may the faithful be blessed and may your Church continue to increase, through Jesus Christ, our Lord, through whom are due to you honour, glory, power and worship, with him and the Holy Spirit, the life-giver, consubstantial with you, now and forevermore. Amen.

At the conclusion of the Catholic Epistle in Arabic, the choir sings the following:

God removes the sins of all through the sacrifice and fragrant smell of incense—even he who offered himself as an acceptable sacrifice upon the Cross for the redemption of us all.

Then the Acts of the Apostles are read, before which the reader says:

The Acts of the Apostles; may their holy blessings be with us.

At the conclusion, the people answer:

The Word of God will endure and be strengthened and confirmed in the Church of God.

The Lesson is then read again in Arabic. At its conclusion the priest, having put incense in the censer, silently says the Prayer of the Acts:

O God, who accepted the sacrifice of Abraham and substituted a lamb instead of Isaac, be pleased to accept from us, O Lord, this sacrifice of incense. In return may we receive the gifts of your mercy and the removal of the corruption of sin, so that we may worthily minister before you in holiness and righteousness for the rest of our life.

Remember, O Lord, the peace of your holy, catholic and apostolic Church.

Deacon :   Pray for the peace of the one, holy, catholic and apostolic Church of God.

The priest kisses the altar on the south side and says :

Which extends from one end of the world to the other. Remember, O Lord, the Patriarch, the Pontiff Abba N.

Deacon :   Pray for our Pontiff, the Pope Abba N. and our Orthodox bishops. Lord, have mercy.

The priest, taking the hand cross, now processes round the altar with the deacon; at each corner of the altar the priest kisses it and says :

Preserve him in safety for many years. Remember, O Lord, our congregation. Bless them.

Deacon :   Pray for this holy church and congregation.

The priest, standing in front of the altar, continues :

Grant, O Lord, that we may retain possession of these churches without any disturbance or hindrance, and that we may retain them according to your will, so that they may be houses of prayer, holiness and blessing. Grant them to us, O Lord, and to your servants who will succeed us, forever.

The deacon now leaves the sanctuary, while the priest continues :

Arise, O Lord, and may your enemies flee away, together with those who hate your holy name.

The priest again processes around the altar, and having arrived at the east side, says :

May your people be blessed many times over, and may they do your will, through the grace and love of mankind that your only-begotten Son, our Lord and Saviour Jesus Christ, holds for us.

The priest processes around the altar for the third time, saying :

Through whom are due to you, with him and the Holy Spirit, the life-giver, who is consubstantial with you, all glory, honour, power and worship forevermore. Amen.

The priest kisses the altar; then he censes it three times, saying :

We adore you, O Christ, and your Father, together with the Holy Spirit, for you have come and saved us.

   I will sing to you before the angels, and will worship in your holy temple.

   As for me, I will worship in your house and in your holy temple.

The priest now censes the icon of the Blessed Virgin three times, saying :

> Hail Mary, the most beautiful dove, which carried the Word of God for us; we greet you with the Archangel Gabriel saying; Hail Mary, full of grace, the Lord is with you. Hail O Virgin, the glory of our race; you have borne Emmanuel for us. We pray that you will remember us before the Lord Jesus Christ, that he will forgive us our sins.

The other icons and then the assembled clergy are censed. During the censing of the choir the priest prays :

> May the blessings of our fathers, the Apostles, and of our father Peter and our master Paul, be upon us. Amen.

The priest then passes through the congregation, censing the people as he goes, saying :

> Jesus Christ is the same yesterday, today and forevermore, in one Person. Let us worship and glorify him.

This prayer is said several times while the priest passes through the body of the church. On his return to the altar, he offers incense, saying :

> O God, who accepted the thief's confession, receive the confession of your people, and forgive them all their sins, for the sake of your holy name and according to your mercy, and not according to the magnitude of our sins.

THE TRISAGION

On some occasions the priest sits during the recitation of the Trisagion. In the Catholic usage the priest prays :

> Holy God, holy Mighty and holy Immortal, have mercy upon us.

In the Monophysite usage he prays :

> O holy God, Mighty and Immortal,
>   have mercy upon us.
> O holy God, Mighty and Immortal,
>   have mercy upon us.
> O holy God, Mighty and Immortal,
>   have mercy upon us.

Choir :   Glory be to the Father and to the Son and to the Holy Spirit, now and forevermore. Amen.

Priest :   Peace be with you *(blesses people with hand cross)*.

People :   And with you.

Priest :　Christ our God, who spoke to the holy disciples and
apostles and said: Many prophets and good men have
wanted to see the things you have seen and have not seen
them, and to hear the words you have heard and have not
heard them; your eyes and ears are blessed, for they see and
hear. May we be made worthy to hear and to do what is
written in your holy Gospels, through the prayers of your
saints.

Deacon :　Let us pay attention to the holy Gospel.

People :　Lord, have mercy.

Priest :　Remember also, O Lord, all those who have asked to be
remembered in our prayers and thoughts. Give rest to
those who have died and health to those who are ill, for you
are our life and our salvation, our hope, health and resurrection. To you we offer the glory, honour and worship,
with your good Father, and the Holy Spirit, the life-giver,
who is consubstantial with you, now and forevermore.
Amen.

*Next a psalm is usually recited. The priest ascends the altar and censes it.
After the psalm the Book of Gospels is brought to him by the deacon, who
holds it open while the priest proceeds to cense it, saying in a low voice :*

Kiss the Gospel of Jesus Christ, the Son of God; may glory
be given to him forevermore.

*The priest, followed by the deacon holding the open book, processes around
the altar, saying in a low voice :*

O Lord, now let your servant go in peace according to your
promise, because I have seen the salvation which you had
prepared for us, a Light to inspire us and to be the glory of
your people Israel.

Deacon :　Stand in awe and listen to the holy Gospel.

*The priest and deacon leave the sanctuary; the priest then censes the book,
saying :*

Kiss the Gospel of Jesus Christ, the Son of God; may glory
be given to him forevermore.

*The priest then proffers the book to the other priests to kiss, saying to each
of them 'Kiss the Gospel . . .'; then he kisses it himself, saying the same
prayer. He then raises his voice to say :*

Blessed is he who comes in the name of the Lord.

Deacon :　O Lord, bless the reading from the holy Gospel according
to N.

People :   Glory be to you, O Lord.

Deacon :   Stand in fear of God and listen to the holy Gospel according to N.

Priest :   The Lord God and Saviour of us all, Jesus Christ, the Son of the living God; may glory be given to him forevermore.

The Gospel is then read. At its conclusion the priest says :

    Glory be to God forevermore.

The Gospel is censed while the priest says the following prayer silently :

    And to you everyone should offer praise, together with the glory, honour, power and worship we offer you with your Father and the Holy Spirit, the life-giver, who is consubstantial with you, now and forevermore. Amen.

People :   Forevermore.

At this stage it is customary to read the Gospel in Arabic. It is read either by the deacon or priest. The sermon follows.

Choir :   Blessed be the Father, the Son and the Holy Spirit, the perfect Trinity; we worship and glorify him.

The priest then enters the sanctuary, ascends the altar, kisses it and half turning towards the people blesses them, saying :

    Peace be to you all.

People :   And with you.

Priest :   Again let us pray to God the Father Almighty, the Father of our Lord God and Saviour Jesus Christ. We pray and beg your goodness, O Lover of mankind. Remember, O Lord, the peace of your one, holy, catholic and apostolic Church.

Deacon :   Let us pray for the peace of the one, holy, catholic and apostolic Orthodox Church of God.

People :   Lord, have mercy.

Priest :   Which extends from one end of the world to the other. Bless all nations and countries and give us that peace which is from heaven, as well as a peaceful life. Give grace to the kings of this Christian world, the armies and governments that preserve peace. Fill them with your peace, O King of peace, and grant us the favour of your presence. As you have given us everything, take us for yourself. We call upon your holy name and may our lives be imbued with your Holy Spirit and may we not be conquered by the dominion of sin.

People :   Lord, have mercy.

Priest :   Let us pray again to God Almighty, the Father of our Lord God and Saviour Jesus Christ, that we might beg your goodness, O Lover of mankind. O Lord, remember also our Patriarch and our Archbishop Abba N.

Deacon :   Pray for our Pontiff the Pope Abba N., pope and patriarch, as well as for our Orthodox bishops.

People :   Lord, have mercy.

Priest :   Preserve him safely, for many years of peace, so that he may complete his pontificate according to your will, rightly directing your people in truth and holiness, together with all Orthodox bishops, priests and deacons. May they be granted your peace and salvation. Receive all the prayers which we offer up to you for ourselves and for all your people everywhere.

The priest then puts incense into the censer, and while holding it in his right hand he says :

Receive our prayers upon your altar in heaven as a sweet fragrance. Speedily eradicate all our enemies, visible and invisible, and be pleased to preserve your faithful in peace and righteousness.

People :   Lord, have mercy.

Priest :   O Lover of mankind, we pray and beg your goodness to remember the sacrifice and thanksgivings to the honour and glory of your holy name that we have offered.

Deacon :   Pray for them who have provided the sacrifices, the wine, the oil, the incense, the holy vessels of the altar, so that Christ, our God, might repay them in heaven. May he forgive us our sins.

Monophysite Copts observe the following forms.

People :   Lord, have mercy.

The priest offers incense until he concludes the following prayer :

Receive them upon your altar in heaven as a sweet fragrance before your majestic throne in heaven, by the ministry of your angels and archangels. Just as you accepted the offerings of Abel and Abraham and the widow's pence, likewise be pleased to accept the offerings of your servants, rich and poor, seen and unseen. Grant them things that do not decay for their corruptible gifts, things eternal for things temporal, and may their houses be filled with goodness.

By the power of your archangels and angels, may they be defended. Just as they have remembered your holy name here on earth, be pleased, O Lord, to remember them in your kingdom and do not allow them to be abandoned in this world.

People : Lord, have mercy.

Priest : Again let us pray to God Almighty, the Father of our Lord God and Saviour Jesus Christ. We pray and beg of your goodness, O Lover of mankind, to remember our congregations. *(The priest blesses the people :)* ✠ Bless them.

Deacon : Pray for this holy church and for our congregations. Amen.

People : Lord, have mercy.

Priest : Grant that we may direct them according to your holy and blessed will and may our churches become *(he stretches out his hand over the altar holding the veil)* houses of prayer *(he stretches out his hand westward)* houses of holiness *(northwards)* houses of blessing *(southwards)* ✠ may we be granted their possession; so also our successors.

The priest then offers incense three times over the altar, saying :

O Lord God, may all your enemies flee, together with those who hate your holy name.

The priest then faces towards the West and incenses the people three times, and then the deacon(s); he then turns to the East and offers incense three times, saying :

May your people be blessed many times over, and may they always do your will, through the grace and mercies and love of your only Son, our Lord and Saviour Jesus Christ.

At the mention of the name of Jesus, the priest offers incense three times towards the altar, and continues :

Through whom are due to you, with him and the Holy Spirit, the life-giver, who is consubstantial with you, all the glory, honour, power and worship, forevermore. Amen.

The priest censes the assistant priest and then the censer is handed to the deacon, who says :

Let us attend. Lord, have mercy; Lord, have mercy.

Priest and people then recite the Nicene Creed, with the 'Filioque', of course. At its conclusion, the priest washes his hands three times, saying :

Wash me, that I may be made whiter than snow. May I hear of joy and happiness, and may those who are distressed, rejoice. In innocence I will wash my hands and will process around your altar, O Lord, in order that I might hear your praises.

The priest faces West and dries his hands before the people; he then blesses them:

> Peace be to you all.

People :   And with you.

The priest recites the Prayer of the kiss (St Basil):

> O great and eternal God, who created man and by the humanity of your only Son, our Lord God and Saviour Jesus Christ, destroyed that death which was introduced into this world by the envy of the devil; you have filled the world with heavenly peace, for which all the angelic hosts praise and glorify you. Glory to God on high and peace on earth towards men of goodwill.

Deacon :   Pray for perfect love and peace, and the kisses of the holy Apostles.

People :   Lord, have mercy.

Priest :   Out of your goodness, O God, fill our hearts with your peace and remove every guilty stain of hypocrisy and sin; eradicate also the memory of our falls and so make us worthy, O Lord, to greet one another with a holy kiss *(The Pax is given by the priest approaching the deacon and embracing him)* that we might share without condemnation the immortal and heavenly gifts of Christ our Lord. Through whom are due to you, with him and the Holy Spirit, the life-giver, consubstantial with you, all the glory, honour, power and worship forevermore. Amen.

Deacon :   Salute one another with a holy kiss.

The people say three times:

> Lord, have mercy upon us. Amen. Jesus Christ, hear us and have mercy.

THE CANON

The priest now removes the great veil from the bread and wine, waves the veil over his head, and then places it on the right-hand side of the altar, while the deacon says:

> Offer, offer, offer; let us stand in fear and trembling, and while looking eastward, may we attend this sacrifice of praise.

People :   A sacrifice of praise.

The priest now turns towards the people and blesses them:

> ✠ The Lord be with you all.

People :   And with you.

Turning towards the deacon, the priest continues :

✠ Lift up your hearts.

People :   Let us lift them up to the Lord.

The priest blesses himself and continues :

✠ Let us give thanks to the Lord.

People :   Because it is right and worthy.

Priest :   Right and worthy it is. Who is the Lord God of righteousness and who is eternally King and who was before all time,
who created everything in heaven and earth. The Father of
our Lord God and Saviour Jesus Christ, who created everything by him, the things which are seen and those which are
not seen; who sits upon the throne of his glory and is
worshipped by all the holy powers.

Deacon :   All those who are sitting, stand up.

Priest :   Around whom the angels stand, together with the archangels, the principalities, the powers, the thrones, the
dominations and the Virtues.

Deacon :   Look to the East.

Priest :   For around you stand the full-eyed cherubim and the six-
winged seraphim, who sing unceasingly and unfailingly.

*The people recite one of several Responsories; the following is the most
common :*

O heaven, rejoice! O Earth, sing aloud! The cherubim have
spread their wings and cry to you three times—

Priest :   Holy, holy, holy are you, O Lord. Alleluia. Glory be to the
Father and to the Son and to the Holy Spirit. As it was, is
now and shall be forevermore. Amen.

The priest and choir sing the following together :

The cherubim and seraphim shout aloud, crying: Holy,
holy, holy is the Lord God of Sabaoth; heaven and earth
are full of your glory.

*The priest removes the chalice veil, and with it and the hand cross he blesses
himself, the deacon and the people. He then replaces the veil and cross upon
the altar. He prays :*

Truly the Lord God is holy, holy, holy. He created us and
put us in the Garden of Eden, where we broke his commandment through the devil's tempting. Having forgone

eternal life, we were thrown out of the Garden of Eden, but you did not forsake us entirely, as you guided us by your holy prophets. Finally when we were in the darkness of ignorance and the shadow of death you enlightened us through your only Son, our Lord God and Saviour Jesus Christ; who by the operation of the Holy Spirit and the virgin Mary *(the people interject: 'Amen.')* took flesh and became man and directed us on the way to salvation. He gave us the birth from heaven through water and the Spirit and united us to himself, having been sanctified by the Holy Spirit. He loved us and gave himself up to death for our salvation from the sentence which had hung over us on account of our sins. He went into paradise from the Cross *(The people interject: 'Amen. I believe.')* and rose again from the dead on the third day, and ascended into heaven, where he sat at the right hand of God the Father. He has appointed a day of judgment, on which day he will judge the world, and when every man will be rewarded or punished according to his works.

People :   O Lord, according to your mercy and not on account of our sins.

The deacon presents the censer to the priest, who places incense in it and then places his hands in the smoke and continues :

And he instituted this great mystery of godliness.

The priest then extends his hands over the bread and wine, saying :

For when he was determined to surrender himself up to death, for the life of the world . . .

People :   We believe; we believe that it is true. Amen.

The priest then takes the bread in his hands :

He took bread into his pure, spotless, holy and blessed life-giving hands . . .

People :   I believe that this is true indeed. Amen.

The priest raises his eyes :

He looked up to heaven, to you, O God, who are his Father and Lord of all . . .

The priest takes the bread in his left hand, and makes the sign of the cross over it with his right, saying :

He gave thanks ✠

People :   Amen.

The priest blesses it again, saying :

> He blessed it ✠

People :   Amen.

The priest blesses it a third time ✠ *He sanctified it.*

People :   Amen. Amen. Amen. Amen. We believe, confess and glorify
him.

*The priest then breaks the bread slightly on one side, and holding it in his
hands and looking at it, says :*

> He broke it and gave it to his holy disciples and apostles,
> saying: Take, eat you all of it. This is my body, which shall
> be broken for you and for many, to be given for the remission
> of sins . . .

*The priest places the bread on the paten; if he is a Catholic, he kneels and
rises. From now on, the priest holds the thumb and forefinger joined. He
then continues :*

> Do this as a remembrance of me.

People :   We believe that this is so. Amen.

*The priest then uncovers the chalice and touching the lip of it with the joined
thumb and forefinger of his right hand says :*

> He tasted and gave it also to his holy disciples and apostles,
> saying *(he tilts the chalice)*: Take and drink all of it, for this
> is my blood of the New Testament, which shall be shed for
> many, to be given for the remission of sins. Do this in
> memory of me.

*The priest then covers the chalice and worships the sacred species, while
the people respond :*

> Amen. This we believe it to be. Amen.

The priest, pointing at the host, says :

> For as often as you eat this bread *(pointing at the chalice)* and
> drink this cup, you commemorate my death and resurrection.

People :   Amen. Amen. Amen. We commemorate your death, O Lord,
and we acknowledge your holy resurrection and ascension.
We praise and bless you; we thank and entreat you, O our
God.

The priest says silently :

> We commemorate his holy passion and his resurrection and
> ascension; we also commemorate his sitting at the right hand
> of God, the Father and of his second coming from heaven,
> full of glory. We offer to you these your gifts of your gifts.
> *(He raises his voice :)* Of all, and for all, and in all.

Deacon :   In fear and trembling, let us worship God.

People :   We praise, bless, serve and worship you.

The priest says inaudibly :

We your sinful and unworthy servants worship and beg you, O Christ our God, by the beneficence of your mercy, to grant that your Holy Spirit may descend upon us and these gifts here and that they may be purified *(he raises his voice)* and may make them appear as a sanctification of your saints.

Deacon :   Let us pay attention. Amen.

The priest, making the sign of the cross three times over the host, says :

And make this ✠ bread the holy body of . . .

People :   I believe.

Priest :   Our Lord, ✠ God and Saviour Jesus Christ, which is given for the remission of sins ✠ and eternal life to those who receive it.

People :   Amen.

The priest makes the sign of the cross three times over the chalice :

And this cup, ✠ the glorious Blood of the New Testament of . . .

People :   I believe.

Priest :   Our Lord, ✠ God and Saviour Jesus Christ, which is given for the remission ✠ of sins and eternal life to those who receive it.

People :   Amen. Lord, have mercy; Lord, have mercy; Lord, have mercy.

Priest :   Make us worthy, O Lord, to receive your holy things for the sanctification of our souls, bodies and spirits, that we may be one body and one spirit, and that we may be united with all the saints, who have pleased you. Remember, O Lord, your holy, catholic and apostolic Church.

Deacon :   Pray for the holy, catholic and apostolic Orthodox Church of God . . .

People :   Lord, have mercy.

Priest :   Which you have purchased with the glorious Blood of Christ. Preserve her in peace with all the Orthodox bishops, who are in her. Remember, O Lord, our blessed father, the glorious Pope Abba N., as well as his Bishop Abba N.

Deacon :   Pray for our Pope Abba N. and for our Orthodox bishops.

People :   Lord, have mercy.

Priest :   As well as those who, with them, correctly define the truth. May they feed your flock in peace for many years. Remember, O Lord, the abbots, together with all Orthodox priests and deacons.

Deacon :   Pray for the priests, deacons and subdeacons of the Church, together with all the seven orders in the Church of God.

People :   O God, the Father Almighty, have mercy upon us.

Priest :   As well as all your ministers and faithful people. In your mercy, O Lord, remember us all as well as the integrity of this holy place and all the places of our Orthodox fathers.

Deacon :   Let us pray for the safety of the world, this city and every city, all lands, islands and monasteries.

People :   Lord, have mercy.

Priest :   And those who dwell in these places in the faith of God; be pleased also, O Lord, to give us favourable weather and fruitfulness of the earth.

Deacon :   Let us pray for favourable weather and fruitfulness of the earth, so that Christ our God will bless the earth and that our sins will be forgiven.

People :   Lord, have mercy; Lord, have mercy; Lord, have mercy.

Priest :   May everything flourish according to your plan and goodness, and so make the earth a happy and fruitful place, with the time of sowing and harvesting beneficently ordered. We beg you for the sake of the poor, the widows, orphans, strangers and wanderers, and for us all who hope in you and call upon your holy name, that you will be generous towards us, and that our hearts will be filled with joy and happiness and that we will always have sufficient according to our needs.

People :   Lord, have mercy.

Priest :   Remember, O Lord, those who have brought these gifts to you, as well as those for whom these gifts have been brought; grant them a heavenly reward.

Deacon :   Pray over these gifts and sacrifices, and for them who have brought them.

Priest :   O Lord, let us remember our obligation to participate in the commemoration of your saints. O Lord, graciously remember all those saints who have pleased you from the beginning of the world, especially our holy fathers, the patriarchs, the prophets, apostles, preachers, evangelists, martyrs and confessors, as well as all those who lived a perfect life of faith, especially the glorious virgin mother of God, the holy Mary, together with John the Baptist, holy Stephen, the first deacon and martyr, the Evangelist Mark, apostle and martyr, the holy Patriarch Athanasius, who was like an apostle, as well as Cyril, Basil and Gregory, together with our righteous father, the great Abba Antony and the other abbots Paul, Marcarius and Macarius, as well as the whole choir of the saints, through whose prayers and entreaties on our behalf be pleased to grant us mercy and for the sake of your holy name, deliver us.

Deacon :   Let us pray that the Lord will grant rest to our fathers the patriarchs who have died, and may we receive the forgiveness of our sins.

The deacon then reads out the list of the departed, while the priest continues inaudibly the following prayer :

Remember also, O Lord, all those who have died. Grant all our deceased priests and lay people eternal rest in Abraham's bosom together with Isaac and Jacob. May they receive refreshment in the paradise where all sorrow and sadness have been dispelled.

Incense is then placed in the censer. Meanwhile the priest takes the chalice veil in his right hand and with his left hand on the altar, he half turns towards the people, saying :

God have mercy upon us and bless ✠ us and may his face shine upon us and be merciful to us. O Lord, grant salvation to your people, sustain them and may the repute of all Orthodox Christians everywhere be enhanced.

Through the prayers and entreaties which our Lady, the holy mother of God, the blessed virgin Mary continually makes for us, as well as the prayers of the three mighty archangels Michael, Gabriel and Raphael, together with the four immaterial living creatures with the twenty-four elders and all the angelic choir; their prayers joined by those of the heavenly armies together with the entreaties of the patriarchs and prophets, the apostles and martyrs, with the just and righteous and all holy virgins; and through the blessing of the angel of this holy Sacrifice, as well as the blessing of the holy mother of God and the blessing of the day of the Lord, may we be assisted by their power and grace and so be continually in their company. Amen.

The priest then makes the sign of the cross over the people with the veil and returns to face the altar. The deacon prays :

The great Abba Antony, together with the righteous Paul

and the abbots Marcarius and Macarius, with Abba John the Short, Abba Pishwi, Abba Paul, Abba Isidore, Abba Moses, Abba Pachom and Abba Paphnutius, as well as all who have taught the truth, the Orthodox bishops, priests, deacons, clerics and layfolk—may we be assisted by their grace.

People :   Glory to you, O Lord, and have mercy upon us. Lord, have mercy; give us your blessing and spare us. Amen.

The priest then places incense in the censer.

O Lord, grant eternal rest to them who have died, and may we have the grace to persevere in the faith and continue peacefully until our life's end.

People :   As it was, is now and shall be forevermore. Amen.

Priest :   So that as in this and in everything, the holy name will be extolled, together with your blessed Son, Jesus Christ and the Holy Spirit. Peace be to you all.

People :   And with you.

The priest recites the Preface of the Fractions :

Let us give thanks to God Almighty, the Father of our Lord God and Saviour Jesus Christ, because he has made us worthy to stand before him here and to raise our hands, so as to minister to his holy name. Let us then beg him, so that he will make us even worthier to participate in the communion of his divine and unending Mysteries.

People :   Amen.

The priest then takes the bread in his hands, saying :

The holy body. *(He then raises it above the chalice, saying :)* And the glorious blood of his Christ, he the Almighty Lord our God.

Deacon :   Amen. Amen. Let us pray. Lord, have mercy.

Priest :   Peace be to you all.

People :   And with you.

The priest then kneels and worships the Blessed Sacrament, rises, takes the sacred host and breaks off a particle. From this piece he breaks off a smaller particle, and replaces the whole on the paten, saying :

The Lord God, who gives light to the world, and who has crowned us in the faith, and who gives us whatever we need before we ask, grant us the grace to be acceptable to you and to confidently beg you, our holy Father in heaven, to say . . .

The people recite the 'Our Father'. The priest says inaudibly :

> We also pray you, O good Father, lover of goodness, that we may not be led into temptation nor become subject to the dominion of sin, but that we may be delivered from all evil. Rebuke the devil who tempts us and may all occasions of sin be removed from us, through your holy power. *(Aloud:)* Through Jesus Christ our Lord.

Deacon :   Let us bow down our heads before the Lord.

People :   Before you, O Lord.

The priest prays inaudibly :

> Your only Son, our Lord God and Saviour Jesus Christ, has been so bountiful towards us; we have confessed his saving passion, we have told of his death and believed in his resurrection. We give you thanks for all the mercy you have shown us and may we be prepared to look upon those things which the angels long to look upon. We pray and beg of your goodness, O Lover of mankind, to sanctify us and join us to yourself through the communion of the holy Mysteries, so that we may become imbued with your holy Spirit and fortified in the faith; may we speak of your glory forevermore. *(Aloud:)* Through Jesus Christ our Lord.

Deacon :   Let us fearfully wait on God.

Priest :   Peace be to you all.

People :   And with you.

The priest silently prays the Prayer of Absolution to the Father :

> Lord God Almighty, Healer of our souls, bodies and spirits, you are he who spoke to our father Peter by the mouth of your only Son, our Lord God and Saviour Jesus Christ, saying: 'You are Peter, and upon this rock I will build my Church, and the gates of hell will not prevail against it; and I will give to you the keys of the kingdom of heaven, that whatever you bind on earth will be bound in heaven, and whatever you loose on earth will be loosed in heaven.' Therefore, O Lord, let the misery of your servants, my fathers, brethren and myself, your unworthy servant, be loosed by my mouth, through your holy, good and loving Spirit. O God, you who remove the sins of the world, be prepared to accept the penitence of your servants for the forgiveness of their sins, because you are a compassionate and merciful God. If we have sinned either by word or deed, spare us and forgive us out of your goodness and love of mankind; O God, absolve us and all your people.

The priest then takes the little veil in his right hand, standing half turned towards the people, with his right hand extended towards them and his left hand on the altar; he then says the following inaudibly (Monophysites only):

> O Lord, remember your servants, all Orthodox Christians throughout the world; those who are alive maintain in life, and to those who are dead grant eternal rest. Remember, O Lord, the children of the Church, the abbots, priests, deacons, clerics and all layfolk; those who are alive be pleased to maintain by the angel of peace, and to those who have died grant eternal rest.
>
> Remember also, O Lord, all sick people and heal them. Keep and bless all those who are assembled together here in this church; remember our fathers and our brethren who are absent and bring them home in peace; remember all those who suffer or who are in any way afflicted and deliver them, O Lord. Remember also, O Lord, all those who have requested a remembrance in our prayers; may they be remembered in your heavenly kingdom.
>
> Remember also, O Lord, my father, my mother and brethren as well as my spiritual fathers; those who are alive maintain by the angel of peace, and to those who have died grant eternal rest.
>
> O Lord, remember also my lowliness; eradicate my many sins and where sin has abounded may your grace flourish instead. Do not allow my sins and failings to deprive your people of the grace of your Holy Spirit. Deliver us and your people from every sin, curse, denial and heresy. O Lord, be pleased to grant us the grace always to do what is most pleasing to you. May our names be inscribed in the heavenly roll of the saints . . .

If the liturgy is celebrated after a Catholic fashion, the following prayer is substituted instead of the fore-going:

Priest: Absolve us and all your people, from all sin, curses, apostacies, perjuries and dealings with the heretics and heathen, and O Lord, always be pleased to grant us the grace to do what ever pleases you most. May our names be inscribed in the heavenly roll of the saints.

The priest then uncovers the chalice, while continuing aloud:

In the kingdom of heaven, through Jesus Christ, our Lord.

Deacon: Let us attend with fear.

People: Lord, have mercy. Lord, have mercy. Lord, have mercy.

The priest then takes the particle detached at the Fraction, and raising it above his head, says:

The Holy to the holy.

The particle is then lowered, and the priest makes the sign of the cross with it over the chalice, saying :

Blessed be the Lord Jesus Christ, the Son of God. He has blessed it by his Holy Spirit. Amen.

Deacon : Amen. One holy Father. One holy Son. One Holy Spirit. Amen.

The priest then intincts the particle with the precious blood and says :

Peace be to you all.

People : And with you.

The priest then touches the rest of the sacred host with the intincted particle, saying :

The holy body and the precious blood of Jesus Christ, the Son of God. Amen.

People : Amen.

The priest again signs the chalice with the particle, saying :

The holy, precious body and the very blood of Jesus Christ, the Son of God. Amen.

People : Amen.

The particle is then dropped into the chalice, which is then covered. The priest says :

Truly, this is the body and blood of Emmanuel our God. Amen.

People : Amen. I believe.

Priest : Amen. Amen. Amen. I believe. I believe. I believe and confess to my dying day that this is the life-giving flesh, which your only Son, our Lord God and Saviour Jesus Christ *(the priest takes the paten in both hands and lifts it)* took from our Lady, the holy mother of God, the virgin Mary, which he united with his divinity, without any confusion or alteration; he made a good confession before Pontius Pilate and gave up his body on the Cross, voluntarily for us all. I believe that his divinity was never separated from his manhood not even for one moment, giving it for us for salvation and remission of sins and eternal life to those who receive it. I believe. I believe that this is beyond doubt his body. Amen.

The paten is then moved crosswise and replaced upon the altar. The priest kisses the altar three times, while the deacon says the following :

> Amen. Amen. Amen. I believe. I believe. I believe without a doubt that this is his body. Amen. Pray for us and all those Christians who have asked us to remember them. May the love and peace of Jesus Christ be with you. Let us sing.

The priest prays inaudibly : All glory, honour and worship are eternally due to the Holy Trinity, the Father, Son and Holy Spirit, forevermore, worlds unceasing. Amen.

Meanwhile the choir, accompanied by cymbals, sings the following :

> Alleluia. Praise God in his saints. Alleluia. Praise him in the heavenly expanse of his power. Alleluia. Praise him in his mighty deeds. Alleluia. Praise him according to the magnitude of his greatness. Alleluia. Praise him with the sound of trumpets. Alleluia. Praise him with psalms and the sound of the harp. Alleluia. Praise him with dances and timbrels. Alleluia. Praise him with strings and organ. Alleluia. Praise him with crashing cymbals. Alleluia. Praise him with joyful cymbals. Alleluia. Let everything that breathes praise the name of the Lord our God. Alleluia. Glory be to the Father and to the Son and to the Holy Spirit, as it was, is now and shall be forevermore, worlds unceasing. Amen.

The priest prays inaudibly : O God, grant us remission and forgiveness of our sins, which we have committed willingly and unwillingly, knowingly and unknowingly *(he strikes his breast)*. O Lord, forgive us. Lead us to eternal life, O eternal King, the Word of God the Father of our Lord God and Saviour Jesus Christ. O you, the very bread which has come down from heaven, the giver of life to all who receive, make us worthy without condemnation to consume your holy body and blood. May our reception of your holy Mysteries unite us to you forever.

> You are the Son of God; to you and with him and the Holy Spirit, the life-giver, may glory be given forever. Amen. O Lord, make us all worthy to receive your holy body and blood, for the sanctification of our souls and bodies and the forgiveness of our sins and omissions, that we may be fully united with you forever. Glory be to you, with your good Father and the Holy Spirit, forever. Amen.

Among the Monophysites the following prayer is said by the priest inaudibly and in Arabic :

> O our Lord Jesus Christ, make us worthy to receive your holy body and blood, and may it not be to our condemnation,

but as you said to your holy disciples: 'Take my body and my blood for the remission of your sins', so may we be allowed to have communion with your holy disciples, that by partaking of the life-giving Mysteries we may receive the remission of our sins and the forgiveness of our errors, together with the purification of our souls, bodies and spirits, so that we may finally be confirmed in the faith of your holy name until our dying day, through the intercession of the most pure virgin Mary and all your saints. Amen.

If the liturgy is celebrated according to the Catholic usage, the following prayer is substituted for the Monophysite prayer 'O our Lord Jesus Christ, make us worthy . . .'

Priest :   O Heavenly King make us worthy to receive your holy body and blood for the sanctification of our souls and bodies, for the forgiveness of our sins and offences, so that we may be united with you in body and spirit. Glory be to you together with your Holy Father and Holy Ghost, forevermore. Amen.

The priest then receives the small particle of the sacred host, saying :

This is indeed the body of Emmanuel our God. Amen.

The priest usually meditates a while; then the chalice is uncovered, the priest raises it, moves it crosswise and consumes part of the sacred blood with the particle, saying :

This is indeed the body and blood of Emmanuel our God. Amen.

The priest then meditates a while again, and then he takes the paten and faces the people, saying aloud :

Lord, I am not worthy that you should come under my roof, but only say the word and my soul will be healed.
     The Holy to the holy; Blessed be the Lord Jesus Christ, the Son of God, who has blessed (it) by his Holy Spirit. Amen.

Communicants may approach at this point, and to each the priest says :

This is indeed the body and blood of Emmanuel our God. Amen.

The communicants used to reply, 'Amen. I believe.' After all have been communicated, the priest moves the paten crosswise in the direction of the people; he turns and replaces the paten on the altar, consuming what remains of the sacred host, saying :

This is indeed the body of Emmanuel our God. Amen.

The priest then cleans the paten into the chalice and consumes the remains of the precious blood, saying :

> This is indeed the body and blood of Emmanuel our God. Amen.

The deacon pours water into the chalice, while the priest says :

> Peace be to you all.

People :   And with you.

The contents of the chalice are then consumed. Wine and water are then poured over the priest's fingers into the chalice, and this he also drinks. The chalice is then wiped clean and covered suitably, during which the priest silently recites the following prayer in Arabic :

> Our mouth is full of gladness and joy, because we have been partakers of your immortal Mysteries, O Lord. For those things which the eye has not seen nor the ear heard nor the heart experienced, have been prepared for those who love your holy name. And you have revealed them to the children of your Church, as it seemed good to you, because you are so merciful. To you, O Father, together with your Son and the Holy Spirit, we offer glory, honour and worship, forevermore, worlds unceasing. Amen.

The priest recites the Prayer of Inclination after Communion :

> O Lord, be with those servants of yours who minister before you and who supplicate your holy name. Assist them by your presence and aid them in their good works. Raise their hearts above every base desire and grant that they may live and meditate on the things of eternity and so understand the things relating to you; through your only Son, our Lord God and Saviour Jesus Christ, to whom we and all your people cry aloud, saying: O God our Saviour, have mercy upon us.

Among the Monophysites the priest now leaves the sanctuary and facing the people with outstretched arms says the Prayer of Benediction :

> God, have mercy upon us and bless us. May his face shine upon us and be merciful to us. O Lord, save your people and bless your heritage. Sustain them and may the repute of all Orthodox Christians everywhere be enhanced through the prayers and entreaties which our Lady, the holy mother of God, the blessed virgin Mary, continually makes for us, as well as the prayers of the three mighty archangels, Michael, Gabriel and Raphael, together with the twenty-four elders and all the angelic choir. May their prayers be joined by those of the heavenly armies, together with the

entreaties of the patriarchs and prophets, the apostles and martyrs, with the just and the righteous and all holy virgins. Through the blessing of the angel of this holy Sacrifice, and the blessing of the mother of God, the holy virgin Mary, as well as the blessing of the Lord's day, may we be assisted by their powers and grace and sustained by their help forevermore. Amen. O Christ, our God and King of Peace, grant us your peace; may it always remain with us, because to you are due the power and the glory and blessing forevermore. Amen.

The Our Father is then recited. Among the Catholic Copts the priest says the following prayers :

O Lord, save your people and bless your heritage; govern them and may they be exalted forever; may they preserve the faith in honour and glory until their lives' end. Keep them in that charity which surpasses all human comprehension and in that peace which is beyond all thought.

Through the prayers and petitions which our Lady, the holy Mary, mother of God, the saint of the day, and all heavenly armies, make for us all.

O Christ, King of Peace, our God, give us your peace and confirm us in it, for to you are ascribed the power, glory, honour and might, forevermore. Amen. Depart in peace.

The Lord's Prayer is recited, with outstretched arms, following which the priest faces the congregation and with the hand cross gives the following blessing :

May the almighty and merciful God, Father, Son and Holy Spirit, bless ✠ you, through the intercession of saint N. Amen. Depart in peace.

The priest descends from the altar and recites Psalm 46 :

All you nations, clap your hands in applause; acclaim your God with much happiness. The Lord is over us and worthy of dread, as he is the sovereign ruler of the earth, having tamed all the nations to our will and brought the gentiles to our feet, and claimed us as his own, Jacob the fair, the well-beloved. God ascends with cries of joyous victory; God goes up as the trumpets loudly peal. A psalm, a psalm for our God; a psalm, a psalm for our King. God is King of all the earth, sound the hymn of praise. God reigns over the heathen and sits enthroned in holiness. The rulers of the world throw in their lot with us who worship the God of Abraham, because the powers of our God are so exalted over all the earth.

Deacon :   The grace of our Lord God and Saviour Jesus Christ be
              with you all.

People :   Amen. May it be so forever.

*At the conclusion of these prayers, the priest sprinkles the altar and the
congregation with blessed water. Blessed bread is then distributed. The
priest and assistants retire to the sacristy.*

The Ethiopian Liturgy

INTRODUCTION

I. *General*

The Ethiopian liturgy properly belongs to the Coptic family which derives its origin in the Liturgy of St Mark of Alexandria, but unlike the Coptic liturgy it has retained extensive Syrian influence.

Originally the patriarch of Alexandria exercised jurisdiction over the Ethiopian Christians, and when the Ethiopian Empire was developing, particularly in the thirteenth century, the Church was still very dependent on the Coptic Church, which at that time was trying to excise the influence of Syria. Ironically, the Monophysite heresy, which so beleagured Ethiopia, was received from Egypt and Syria, the very sources of its evangelization.

II. *History*

According to tradition, Christianity was introduced into Ethiopia in the fourth century by St Frumentius and Edesius of Tyre. They had been taken to Ethiopia as prisoners, but having gained the favour of the Emperor at Axum, they were released. Frumentius received episcopal consecration from St Athanasius probably in 350 and subsequently returned to Ethiopia in order to convert it.

The close of the fifth and the beginning of the sixth centuries saw the arrival of the 'Nine Roman (Byzantine) Saints' from Syria; these were probably Syrian Monophysites and came to Ethiopia determined to lay the foundations of the faith in that country.

A cathedral was built at Axum, but as Mohammedanism spread in Africa, so the prosperity of the church declined. About A.D. 640 the patriarchate of Alexandria was transferred to Cairo and the church thus became dependent on the Monophysite patriarch.

Events of the next few centuries are shrouded in doubt. It is known that the Christians were persecuted in the early tenth century, but in 960 the Christian dynasty was established which survived until 1268. Due to the hostility of the neighbouring Mohammedans, the church was without a patriarch on many occasions. Not surprisingly, the corporate morality of the church declined and polygamy was openly indulged in; the greedy and corrupt behaviour of the abunas, or bishops, also left much to be desired.

When the old dynasty was restored in 1268, there was a revival of the church, due in part to the example set by Abuna Takla Haymanot, who was noted for his true asceticism and extraordinary energy.

The end of the thirteenth century saw many attempts to restore full communion with Rome. In fact from the time of the pontificate of Innocent IV (1254) until that of Clement V (1305) there had been feverish missionary activity, but this was doomed due to the fierce opposition of the negus, or emperor.

During the centuries that followed, it was from the Abyssinian Convent in Jerusalem that efforts towards unity with the West were forthcoming. Despite representation at the Council of Florence and the church's acceptance of the Act of Union, very little came of it, because it had been effected without the knowledge of the emperor, Zara Jacob. He had been very active in the reform of the church, by way of improving educational facilities, but many abuses were still allowed, notably polygamy.

With the Mohammedan invasions of 1520–51, there were renewed attempts made towards reunion. It was during the pontificate of Julius III that the efforts of the Jesuits, particularly Fr Peter Paez, produced massive conversions.

In 1614 belief in the two natures of Christ was made mandatory. The Monophysites rebelled, but were quashed. The emperor, Negus Susneyos (Malak Sagad III), renounced polygamy and became a Catholic. He was then excommunicated by Abuna Simeon. In the civil war that followed, Susneyos was victorious and union with Rome was proclaimed in 1626 and Roman Catholicism declared the official religion. This announcement was accompanied by violent enforcement and led to the abdication of Susneyos in 1632. The union came to an end and the accession of Fasilidas saw the banishment of the Jesuits.

Following the expulsion of the Jesuits, the Franciscans attempted to enter the country, bent on its conversion. Their attempts were singularly unsuccessful and earned a crown of martyrdom for many of the friars. In 1894 the Capuchins were able to establish a prefecture in Eritrea, due largely to the accession of Menelik II in 1889. In 1930 Abuna Khidane Mariam Kassa was appointed to be the first bishop of this diocese, which subsequently became established as an exarchate; another exarchate was set up at Addis Ababa.

Among the Monophysites, the Egyptian abuna exercised the powers of primate over the Ethiopian Church. When Abuna Mathew died in 1926, it was Emperor Haile Salassie who began to demand autonomy for the Ethiopian Church and aroused it to assert independence from Egypt. Patriarch John XIX of Alexandria consecrated some bishops for the Ethiopian Church and appointed a Coptic monk, Cyril, to be the Ethiopian abuna.

Ethiopian independence was given a stimulus quite fortuitously by the Italian conquest in 1936, which opened up the country to Western influence. Abba Abraham was nominated to be the patriarch of the new Independent Ethiopian Church; this was arranged by the Viceroy General Graziani. John XIX was naturally incensed by this action and despite inter-governmental negotiations, was compelled to depose and excommunicate the nominated Abba Abraham. Abuna Cyril was restored to office and this saw the renewal of the link with the Coptic patriarchate.

But quite dramatically in 1950 an Ethiopian abuna, Basil, was consecrated by the Coptic Patriarch Joseph II. Though the Egyptian patriarch now exercises a primacy of honour over the Ethiopians, the Ethiopian Church is quite autonomous. Its senior clergy, however, have a vote in the election of the Coptic patriarch and may sit upon any synod or council that may be convened by the Coptic Church.

III. *Calendar*

Naturally enough the basis of the Ethiopian calendar is Coptic. In fact Catholic Ethiopians use the Catholic Coptic calendar, with some local feasts added.

The same feast is sometimes celebrated many times during the course of a year, for example Christmas, which is celebrated on the 24th and 25th of each month, with the notable exception of March.

The annual calendar is similar to that of the Copts. The Gregorian reckoning is employed, which causes New Year's day to fall upon 11 September, or 29 August (Julian reckoning) for the Monophysites.

The fasts observed by the Ethiopians are very similar to those of the Copts, with several minor differences; for example, where the Copts observe fifty-five days of Lenten fasting, the Ethiopians merely observe forty days. The fast of Nineveh is observed by both rites, as is the fast of the Virgin, prior to the feast of the Assumption. The pre-Christmas fast among the Copts is more protracted than it is with the Ethiopians, who merely observe a vigil-style fast.

IV. *Liturgical language and books*

Until recently the liturgical language of the Ethiopian liturgy was Ge'ez, which like Hebrew, Arabic and Syriac is a Semitic tongue. Ge'ez had become what could be considered a learned language and is now gradually being replaced by Amharic, the country's dominant tongue. The use of Amharic in the liturgy is the result of an effort to modernize the church and thus appeal to the new and emerging educated generations, which should prove to be of great assistance to Emperor Haile Selassie in his efforts for his country's good. To date, it is uncertain whether the Catholic Ethiopians will follow suit.

His Grace Abuna Theophilos,
Orthodox Ethiopian A/Patriarch

The Cathedral of Assiut
(Catholic Ethiopian)

The principal books needed for the celebration of the liturgy are the Keddase, which contains the full text of the liturgy, and the Sher'ata-gecāwē (*Ordo Synopseos*), a lectionary.

v.   *The clergy*

Ethiopian Catholics are divided between the jurisdiction of the two exarchs, of Asmara and Addis Ababa, who are appointed with the approval of the Roman See. The clergy are being educated both in Ethiopia and in Rome, and it is quite evident that the future of the Church in Ethiopia lies with the enthusiasm of the laity and the undivided loyalty of the native clergy.

Among the Monophysites, the head of the church is called the catholicos-patriarch; he resides at Addis Ababa. As usual, the patriarch ordains his bishops and consecrates the chrism. Moreover, he would appear to delegate his bishops, as there is no system of fixed dioceses as yet.

There is a form of irregular Monophysite monasticism in existence. The monks appear to follow a variation of the Antonine Rule, but their deplorable lack of education sadly weakens their influence.

vi.   *Church buildings and furnishings*

The interiors of the churches reflect in their extravagance something of the fanciful piety that characterizes the Ethiopian liturgy, unlike the neo-monastic austerity of the Copts. Their rather individual style of music and chant is a further sign of it: to a Western Christian it rather resembles a savage wailing and is usually accompanied by the most unrestrained and exuberant beating of drums and clashing of cymbals, together with an unstinted use of rattles and other noise-making devices.

The churches are often circular and interiorly divided by three concentric circles, enclosing the sanctuary or *kedus kedusan* in the middle.

The second interior division, called the *makdas*, is reserved for the choir and the communicants, while the last division, the *kene mahlet*, is for the bulk of the populace who wish to be present at the liturgy.

The altar is usually square and made of stone or wood. The mensa of the Monophysite altars is composed of hardwood, upon which one finds the *tabot* or ark, which is regarded with great reverence; in fact the tabot in the Cathedral at Axum is reputed to be the original Ark of the Covenant. The blessing of the tabot, which is performed solely by the patriarch, is considered to constitute the consecration of a church. Occasionally the whole altar is referred to as the tabot, but this is quite inaccurate.

Among the Catholic Ethiopians, the tabot is replaced by a tabernacle, in which the Blessed Sacrament is reserved. The mensa of Catholic altars is usually made of stone and covered with silk. The Ethiopians make use of several veils in the liturgy, the *machpad*, which is used to cover the offerings, and the *macdan*, which covers the eucharistic vessels.

VII. *Sacred vessels and eucharistic bread*

The Ethiopic equivalent to a paten is known as the *ained* and measures about seven inches in diameter, while the chalice is of regular dimensions and is known as the *ceuae*.

The altar bread used is a flat, round leavened cake stamped with a cross; the whole surface of the cake is made up of tiny squares set into the corners of the cross. The bread which is to be used in the liturgy must be prepared on the actual day of the celebration and none may be left over. With the notable exception of the Catholics in Eritrea, who always use unleavened bread, Catholic Ethiopians use unleavened bread at 'solemn' liturgies. Among the Monophysites unleavened bread is only used on Holy Thursday.

VIII. *Vestments*

The vestments in common use are Coptic in origin and usually consist of the following:

For a priest, the alb is usually white or coloured silk, as is the amice. The stole is of Byzantine pattern; the girdle only confines the alb. Cuffs are used most extensively and confine the sleeves of the alb. The

Mar Asrate Mariam
Yemmeru, Metropolitan of
Addis Ababa
(Catholic Ethiopian)

vestment or *cappa* (*kabba*) rather resembles a cloak with a hood, which extends from the neck-line to below the knees and is secured at the top.

The cappa of the priest is often ornamented on its upper part with small gold or silver bells, and a shoulder-cape or *lanka* with five short pendants, said to represent the five wounds of Christ. In recent years there has been much variation of style in the design of the cappa.

A deacon usually wears a silk alb, which has very wide sleeves; additionally he may wear a girdle, collar and a cap'pa which is fastened at the breast.

The subdeacon wears a linen alb and girdle with a shorter version of the cappa, and which, like the deacon's, is also secured at the breast.

The taper-bearer wears an alb, over which a girdle, which has been divided crosswise on the breast, is passed and the free ends of the girdle are then thrown over the shoulders.

The T-shaped staff, against which one may rest, is traditionally considered to be a symbol of priestly office.

The outdoor dress of a cleric consists of a cassock over which is worn a wide-sleeved coat like the Byzantine *rason*; a round, flattened cap is also worn.

IX. *Ethiopic versions of the Bible*

The Scriptures were translated into Ge'ez, probably from the Greek, during the fourth and fifth centuries. Both the Old and New Testaments are had in their entirety, but the later surviving texts show a strong influence of Coptic and medieval Arabic versions. Some scholars have suggested that the text of Maccabees is probably from a much later Latin translation.

It is important to note that the Monophysite Ethiopians accept quite a few uncanonical books as being part of the canon of Holy Scripture, for example Enoch, the Apocalypse of Baruch and the Shepherd of Hermas.

X. *Sacraments*

In the administration of the sacraments, the Ethiopians tend to follow closely the Copts, but it is very difficult to get reliable information concerning the details of their usages.

1) *Baptism*—Catholic Ethiopians administer this sacrament with great care, and the order of baptism follows the Coptic practice. But among the Monophysites this sacrament appears to be very carelessly administered; in fact those who embrace the Catholic faith have had to be re-baptized conditionally.

It is a common belief held by the Monophysites that the faith of the parent suffices to save an unbaptized child who dies. Monophysite Ethiopians express a belief in traducianism, which claims that the soul is transferred from the father to the child; this belief serves as an explanation of the origin of the soul.

2) *Confirmation*—The practice of administering confirmation immediately following upon baptism is still practised, and amongst the Monophysites its administration as a distinct sacrament has been lost, probably through a confusion with the anointings associated with the baptismal rite.

3) *Penance*—Catholic Ethiopians seem to be most thorough and circumspect in the administration of this sacrament; however their Monophysite brethren seem to reserve this sacrament for the dying. When a penitent makes his confession in the Monophysite Church, his self-accusation is rarely specific.

4) *The Eucharist*—Among the Catholic Ethiopians, there seems to be a great degree of variety: at a solemn liturgy, both species are received, either separately or by intinction, and the communicant receives them while standing. The words of ministration are: 'The bread of life, which came down from heaven, the body of Christ.' And: 'The cup of life, which came down from heaven, the precious blood of Christ.'

The Monophysite laity rarely receive Communion, and when it is administered it is given under the two species separately. It is now thought that the wine is of doubtful material, because of the lack of care in its manufacture, and the fact that it appears to be made from an infusion of dried grapes.

Some scholars have suggested that the words of institution used in the Monophysite liturgy are quite doubtful: 'Take and eat; this bread is my body.' Similarly: 'This chalice is my blood.'

Because the Monophysites do not reserve the Blessed Sacrament, the Eucharist cannot be given to those who are dying, as is the custom among the Catholic Ethiopians.

Some interesting facts emerge concerning the manner of the celebration of the liturgy among the Catholic Ethiopians; e.g. during the Offertory, which occurs at the beginning of the liturgy, the bread is elevated with the veil. Another Syrian influence can be seen in the blessing of the four quarters of the world and the tilting of the chalice during the Consecration.

5) *Holy Orders*—One feature of the Catholic ordination which will appear peculiar to Western eyes is the fact that the newly-ordained priest (or bishop) does not concelebrate with the ordaining bishop. This practice is held in common with the Syrians and Copts.

Among the Monophysites it is regrettable to have to say that it appears that very little preparation for holy orders is enjoined on prospective priests. Most candidates are married and seem to form a semi-hereditary priestly cast. If Monophysite priests become Catholics, they remain married. Orders are often bestowed on great numbers of men at a time, but this seems to be less frequently the case now. Many scholars rightly hold that Monophysite orders as bestowed in Ethiopia may be invalid.

6) *Marriage*—The ideal of the unity and indissolubillity of marriage is considered by the Monophysites to be above the attainment of most men, and this probably accounts for the frequent occurrence of marital irregularities which though publicly denounced are privately indulged in. Catholic Ethiopians do not seem to be troubled in this respect.

XI. *Conclusion*

During the last three centuries there have been many violent controversies among the Monophysites concerning the 'Unction of Christ', which has split the church into two camps. According to one, Christ as man has become the natural Son of God by the Unction of the Holy Spirit, which divinized his human nature so as to absorb it completely. Others claim that the union of the two natures does not result from the Unction, but is perfected by it.

There is no doubt but that the Monophysite Ethiopians do teach Monophysitism, but many individual clergy do not seem to have a very clear idea of the christology of the Catholic Church.

XII. *Sources of liturgical texts*

Brightman, F. E., *Liturgies Eastern and Western,* Oxford, 1896.
Daoud, M., *Liturgy of the Ethiopian Church,* Addis Ababa, 1954.
Dillman, C. F. A., *Chrestomathia Aethopia,* Leipzig, 1866.
Harden, J. M., *The Anaphoras of the Ethiopic Liturgy,* London, 1928.
Mercer, S. A. B., *Ethiopic Liturgy,* London, 1915.
Semharay, T. M., *La Messe Ethiopienne,* Rome, 1938.

ETHIOPIAN LITURGY

Priest :   In the name of the Father and of the Son and of the Holy Spirit, one God; believing in the Holy Trinity and having recourse to it.

During the recital of the prayers that follow, the deacon recites the prayer 'My brother' which follows after the Prayer of St Basil and before the Prayer of St John Chrysostom. The priest recites the Our Father, Hail Mary and Creed. Psalms 24, 61, 102, 103, 130 and 131 are then recited. The priest continues:

> Lord our God, you alone are holy; you have given holiness to us all by your invisible power, and we entreat you to send the Holy Spirit upon your church, upon this ark and upon all your holy vessels, wherever your holy Mystery is to be celebrated. And now bless your people, set them apart and remove all defilement and uncleanness from them, through the remission of the second birth, so that there is nothing left on them by way of a reminder of their transgressions and pollutions; and be pleased to make this church, this ark and these vessels chosen and cleansed, pure, refined and free from all spots, stains and uncleanness, like the refining of silver from the earth, cleansed, purified and tested; and grant that over them when they are cleansed and purified, the sacrament of the Father and of the Son and of the Holy Spirit may be performed, both now and ever, worlds unceasing. Amen.

The priest enters the sanctuary, prostrates once in front of the veil and says the Prayer of St Basil :

> O Lord, our God and Creator, who has permitted us to enter into this Mystery, who made man through your wisdom and who made him prince over all creatures to rule them in righteousness and truth; grant us the wisdom which dwells in your treasury, purify us, O Lord, and forgive our sins. Our senses and bodies having been purified, may we be so prepared as to approach your sanctuary where we may offer you a sacrifice and a spiritually sweet incense for the forgiveness of your people's sins.
>
> O our Lord and our God and Saviour Jesus Christ, who raised us up from the earth and lifted us from the dust to set us alongside the angels and the princes of your people, make us worthy to serve the words of the holy Gospel

through love, and give us the strength to do your will at this hour. We offer to you a sacrifice of a sweet fragrance and the spiritual fruit which pleases your goodness. Forgive us and be merciful; accept the spotless sacrifice and send down the Holy Spirit upon us and upon this offering which we present so that it may be glorified.

May glory be given to you, the only-begotten Son, our Lord, God and Saviour Jesus Christ, worlds unceasing. Amen.

The deacon meanwhile says the following prayer :

My brother, meditate on your sins and ask for forgiveness so that you may obtain mercy before leaving this church where the pure sacrifice is offered for you and for your brother.

Do not separate yourself from the priest who prays and offers this sacrifice on your behalf, so that you may not go out with the unbaptized who are sent away, but stay within the church and listen to the priest's words, who seeks forgiveness on your behalf and for all sinners so that God may grant forgiveness to everyone.

The meat and drink is our Lord Jesus Christ at his marriage. Blessed be our God who has given us his holy body and precious blood for the forgiveness of sins that more people may obtain eternal life. Glory be to him, worlds unceasing. Amen.

The priest prostrates three times before the altar and recites the Prayer of St John Chrysostom :

O Lord our God, higher than angels and archangels, the dominions and authorities, the cherubim and seraphim, who preceded all creatures in creation, you who are higher than every glory, who raised the humble from the earth and elevated them to the grandure of heaven, who redirected our footsteps for our salvation through your innumerable mercies; O God of mercy and Lover of men, who by the divine will allowed us poor people to know your holy Mystery, may we marvel at your Word; your glory which you have prepared for us is worthy of praise.

O Lord our God, the Good, the Lover of men, who by divine will makes us worthy to enter your holy sanctuary, accept our prayer and render us worthy in true faith to read the Mysteries of your Word which is suitable for your service.

Send the light of your glory upon us, that light which destroys in us all unclean and wicked thoughts and sinful acts. Send us the grace of the Holy Spirit, that fire which destroys the wicked mind and burns up sin.

Make us worthy of this, your holy Mystery. Eradicate all thoughts and lusts which consume our souls so that we may offer a sacrifice that is a heavenly offering without any defilement or stain. Complete this most illustrious and excellent Mystery through the extent of your mercies, compassion and glory.

To you we offer glory, majesty and honour with your benevolent and heavenly Father and with your life-giving Holy Spirit, worlds unceasing. Amen.

The priest prostrates in front of the veil and says the following prayer :

O good and merciful Lord our God, you who dwell with the holy ones and who beneficiently ordered Moses to take blood and sprinkle it on the vessels of the tabernacle, we beg you, O gracious Lover of men, to sanctify these vessels through the Holy Spirit and the sprinkled blood of Jesus Christ so that these vessels will be purified for your service. This rite is a holy rite and truly these Mysteries bestow life.

This is the one holy body and the precious blood of our Lord and Saviour Jesus Christ, because your holy name is holy and full of glory, O holy Trinity, both now and forever, worlds unceasing. Amen.

The priest then recites the following prayer over the vessel coverings :

Our God and our Lord and Saviour Jesus Christ, to whom belong the treasuries, who are full of mercy and pity for the sufferings of mankind, the source of all good things to them that put their trust in you; you who created the heavens out of nothing and gave order to the earth, clouds and sky which remain changeless.

O God and Lover of man, stretch out your hand and may your divine power descend upon these cloths, which will cover your holy body, just as your power descended upon the cloths which enveloped your body in the tomb, and may these cloths be imbued with celestial beauty.

The priest then recites the following prayer over the paten or ained :

O God and our Lord, who stretched out your holy hands on the Cross, lay your holy hands upon this paten which is full of goodness and on which food of a thousand years is prepared by those who love your holy name.

Now also, O Lord and our God, bless and consecrate and purify this paten, which is ablaze with heavenly fire to offer your holy body on this holy altar in this holy, apostolic Church, for to you with the good, heavenly Father and the Holy Spirit, the life-giver, belongs all glory now and evermore, worlds unceasing. Amen.

The priest then recites the following prayer over the bread box or masob :

> O God and our Lord, who said to Moses, your servant on Mount Sinai, 'Make a chosen vessel and place it in front of my tabernacle', now also, Lord and God Almighty, stretch out your holy right hand over this Masob; imbue it with your strength and majesty and with the divine influence of the Holy Spirit, so that it may carry the holy body of your only Son, into this holy apostolic church, for to you with your only Son and the Holy Spirit belongs all glory now and evermore, worlds unceasing. Amen.

The priest bows to the altar once and to the assistant priests and deacon once. The priest then vests, during which the Our Father is recited; this finished, the priest bows three times and recites the following prayer aloud :

> O God, you who know the hearts of all of us, you the Holy One resting among the holy ones, you who alone are sinless, all-powerful and the forgiver of sins, forgive me my sins, O Lord, because you know that as I am a sinner I am unfit to celebrate this holy Mystery and to make sacrifice; out of your store of unending mercy, pardon and absolve all my offences.
>
> Grant me your merciful grace and may your power descend upon me so that I may be made fit to celebrate your holy liturgy according to your will, and may this incense burn most fragrantly.

He places incense into the censer and continues :

> O Lord, be among us and bless us, for you are the forgiver of sins, our guide, our strength, our hope and our protection, and to you, with the Father and the Holy Spirit, we offer thanksgiving, honour and worship, worlds unceasing. Amen.
>
> O Lord our God, who taught us this great Mystery which is for our salvation and who called us to be your servants even though we are unworthy to be ministers at your holy altar, make us worthy in the power of the Holy Spirit to complete this preparation and liturgy, so that without incurring your displeasure in the face of your great glory, we may present a sacrifice of joyful praise and glory in this sanctuary. O Lord and Saviour, dispenser of all graces, grant us the favour that our gift may be considered acceptable in your presence.
>
> O Lord our God, we pray and beg that you will not abandon your people on account of our sins and especially by reason of my foolishness; because these things that we do are holy according to the gift of the Holy Spirit. Through

Jesus Christ, our Lord, to whom with God the Father and God the Holy Spirit, all honour, glory and power are given now and forever, worlds unceasing. Amen.

The following passage is optional :

Alleluia. As for me, I will come into your house because of the immensity of your mercy, and in reverent fear I will worship in your holy temple. I will praise you, O Lord, with my whole heart, for you have heard the words I have spoken.

The veil is withdrawn and the priest, standing at the entrance of the sanctuary, washes his hands but does not dry them. He then continues the prayer :

How awesome is this day and how solemn is this hour in which the Holy Spirit will descend from heaven and sanctify this sacrifice.

In the spirit of tranquillity and respect, stand up and pray that the peace of God be with me and with you all.

People : Amen.

Priest : Alleluia. If there is anyone among you who has entered the church and has not heard the holy Scriptures read and has not waited until the conclusion of the liturgical prayers and has not received the holy Communion, let him be taken outside of the church because he has violated the law of God and has disdained to stand before the King of heaven, the King of body and soul. This has been taught us by the Apostles in their Canons.

The people respond (from Easter until Pentecost Day) :

Alleluia. Joseph and Nicodemus wrapped in linen cloths the body of Jesus Christ, who rose from the dead according to the Scriptures.

The priest usually bearing the breads, moves around the altar, and finally recites the following prayer :

Remember, O Lord, those who offer you this offering and those for whom this offering is made and grant them all their heavenly reward. As you did accept the sacrifice of Abel the Righteous, the sacrifice of our father Abraham and the two mites of the widow, in a like fashion deign to accept the sacrifice of me, your servant, who makes sacrifice today.

Deign to accept the gifts of your servants, whether they be great or small, whether offered secretly or openly, and fill their houses with your good gifts; and just as they remembered your holy name on earth, remember them in your heavenly kingdom and in this world, and never allow them to be abandoned.

People :　You are the pot of gold in which is hidden the manna, the bread which has descended from heaven and gives life to the world.

The priest says the following prayer while taking the host with his wet hand and passing his hand over and upon it :

I have searched for your presence, O Lord, and I will continue to search; please do not turn away from your servant in anger; assist me and do not despise me, O God, my Saviour.

In the Monophysite liturgy the priest says :

Eulogios Kyrios Jesous Christos, Son of God Almighty, hagiasma ton pneumaton, hagios in truth. Amen.

Priest :　Christ, our true God, sign with your hand ✠ and bless with your hand ✠ and hallow ✠ with your power and give goodness to this bread and let it serve for the forgiveness of your people's sins. Amen.

The priest rubs the bread again and blesses it once more. The assistant priest receives the bread in the veil and says the following prayer :

Just as Joseph and Nicodemus wrapped your body in linen clothing and spices and you were pleased, so similarly be pleased with our humble acts.

In less solemn celebrations of the liturgy, the bread is immediately placed on the altar and covered with the veil. The deacon then hands the bread to the priest, who recites the following prayer :

May this consecration, thanksgiving and praise be acceptable to God the Father for the remission of sins, and may power, blessing and holiness be in this church. Amen.

The subdeacon offers three breads to the priest who chooses one; with this bread covered with the veil, the priest processes around the altar preceded by a server holding a candle and followed by the deacon bearing the chalice. As the priest walks around the altar he recites the following prayer :

Lord our God, who accepted the offering of Abel in the desert and of Noah in the ark, of Abraham on the mountain top and of Elias on top of Mount Carmel and of David on the threshing floor of Ornan the Jebusite, and the widow's mite in the sanctuary, be pleased to accept the oblation and offering of your servant N. which he has brought to honour your holy name. May it be an expiation for his sins. Be pleased to grant him recompense in this world and in the world to come, both now and ever, worlds unceasing. Amen.

Deacon :   The Lord is my shepherd, I shall not lack for anything.

The deacon continues the rest of Psalm 23. Meanwhile the assistant priest receives the chalice from the deacon and pours wine into it, as well as a little water. The priest then says the following prayer :

> O Lord and our God Jesus Christ, who were truly made man and who while truly man were also truly God, we beg you to lay your holy hand over this chalice. Bless, consecrate and cleanse it so that it may be prepared fit for your precious blood, so that this *(pointing)* may be for life and forgiveness of sin to those who drink it in faith.
>
> Glory and honour be rendered to the Father and to the Son and to the Holy Spirit, now and ever, worlds unceasing. Amen. Christ, our God, truly our Lord, who went to the wedding when they requested you in Cana of Galilee and who blessed the water and changed it into wine, be pleased to effect a similar change with this *(pointing)* wine which is set before you. Now may it also be blessed, consecrated and purified, so that it may become the life of soul and body at all times.
>
> Father, Son and Holy Spirit, be with us and fill the wine with joy and happiness, for goodness, for life, for salvation and for the remission of sins, for understanding, for healing and for the counsel of the Holy Spirit, now and ever, worlds unceasing. Amen.
>
> May purity, enlightenment and blessing come to them that truly drink of your precious blood. Amen.

The priest says the following prayer over the cross spoon :

> O Lord our God, who prepared the servant Isaiah the prophet so as to be fit to see the seraph with the tongs in his hand, with which he took live coals from the altar and placed them in Isaiah's mouth, in a similar way, O Lord our God, the Father Almighty, lay your hand on this cross spoon prepared for the distribution of the holy body and the precious blood of your only Son, our Lord and Saviour Jesus Christ.
>
> Now, O Almighty God, bless, sanctify and purify it, so that this cross spoon will be filled with the same power and glory as the seraph's tongs. For to you belong all the glory and dominion with your only Son, our Lord Jesus Christ, together with the Holy Spirit, now and ever, worlds unceasing. Amen.

The priest continues the following versicles and responses, making the sign of the cross as indicated, over the breads :

> Blessed be the Lord Almighty ✠.

People :   Amen.

Priest :   And blessed be the only Son, our Lord and Saviour Jesus Christ ✠.

People :   Amen.

Priest :   And blessed be the Holy Spirit, the Paraclete, the comforter and cleanser of us all ✠.

People :   Amen.

The priest will repeat the same versicles as above and sign the wine in a similar way. This having been concluded, the priest recites the following Doxology and both the bread and wine are blessed simultaneously :

> Glory and honour be given to the holy Trinity, the Father, the Son and the Holy Spirit, co-equal Trinity, now and ever, worlds unceasing. Amen.

The priest turns and takes the hand of the assistant priest and says :

> Remember me, my fellow priest.

The assistant priest answers :

> May the Lord sustain your priesthood and accept your sacrifice.

The priest stands erect, faces the East and while stretching out his arms says the following in a loud voice :

> One God is the holy Father.
> One God is the holy Son.
> One God is the Holy Spirit.

People :   The Holy Spirit.

Priest :   Let all nations praise the Lord.

People :   And may everyone give praise to the Lord.

Priest :   For God has displayed great mercy towards us.

People :   And the Lord remains faithful forever.

Priest :   Glory be given to the Father and to the Son and to the Holy Spirit, now and ever, worlds unceasing. Amen.

People :   Glory be given to the Father and to the Son and to the Holy Spirit, now and ever, worlds unceasing. Alleluia.

The Enarxis

Deacon :   Stand up for prayer.

People :   Kyrie Eleison.

Priest :   Peace be with you all.

People :   And with you.

The priest recites the Prayer of Thanksgiving of St Basil:

> We give thanks to you, the source of all good that comes to
> us, the merciful God, the Father of our Lord and our God
> and our Saviour Jesus Christ, because he has protected and
> preserved us, he has sustained us and regards us as his
> children, he has been our defence and champion and has
> enabled us to be present at this sacrifice. Therefore let us
> pray that the Almighty Lord our God preserve us and that
> we always retain his peace.

Deacon :   Pray.

Priest :   O Lord God Almighty, the Father of our Lord and Saviour
Jesus Christ, we offer the most profound thanks for everything that we are and possess, because you have protected
and preserved us, you have sustained us and regard us as
your children, you have been our defence and you have
enabled us to be present at this sacrifice.

Deacon :   We earnestly implore that the Lord show us mercy and
sympathy and that he may receive intercession from his
saints on our behalf, for what is considered necessary for us
at this particular time. May the blessed Lord prepare us to
be able to receive the Mystery worthily and that we might
receive the forgiveness of our sins.

Deacon :   Kyrie Eleison. Kyrie Eleison. Kyrie Eleison.

Priest :   O Lover of man, it is for these reasons that we beg of your
goodness that we might complete this holy day and all the
days of our life in peace and fearful respect of the Lord. May
all envies, trials, satanic temptations, evils and the uprisings
of our enemies, be removed from me ✠ *(blesses himself)*,
from your people ✠ *(blesses the people)* and from this holy
altar ✠ *(blesses the altar)*.

    O God, who gave us power to overcome all evils, grant us
all that is necessary and good for us. Grant, O God, that we
are not tempted beyond our strength and that we may emerge
from the combat with the evil one victoriously, by virtue of
the grace and beneficence of the Lover of man, your only
Son, our Lord and God and Saviour, Jesus Christ, together

with the Holy Spirit, the life-giver, who is co-equal with you, to whom all honour and glory are due, now and ever, worlds unceasing. Amen.

Deacon :   Stand up for prayer.

People :   May the Lord have mercy upon us.

Priest :   Peace be with you all.

People :   And with you.

The priest recites the prayer of the Oblation of the Apostles :

Let us again entreat Almighty God, the Father of our Lord and Saviour Jesus Christ, on behalf of those who bring offerings within the one, holy, catholic Church, whether these offerings are sacrifices, first-fruits, tithes, thanksgivings or memorials, whether great or small, whether secret or manifest. May we also remember those who would like to give but have nothing to give, that he may accept their ready willingness and that through the immensity of his power the heavenly kingdom might be our reward.

Deacon :   Pray for them that bring offerings.

People :   We pray that you accept the offerings of all here present.

The assistant priest then repeats the Prayer of the Oblation of the Apostles. The deacon continues :

Stand up for prayer.

People :   May the Lord have mercy upon us.

Priest :   Peace be with you all.

People :   And with you.

Priest :   O my Lord and Master Jesus Christ, Lover of man, look favourably upon this *(he points at the bread)* bread and upon this *(he points at the chalice)* cup which we have set upon this altar.
Bless this bread ✠, hallow this cup ✠ and cleanse them both ✠. And change this bread *(pointing)* to become your pure body and let what is mingled with this cup *(pointing)* become your precious blood offered for us all; may it be a cure and salvation for body, soul and spirit.
You are the King of the whole world, Christ our God, and to you we offer praise, glory and worship with your heavenly Father and the Holy Spirit, the life-giver, who is co-equal with you, now and forever, worlds unceasing. Amen.

Deacon :   Listen to the commandment of our fathers, the Apostles: 'Let no one entertain in his heart feelings of rancour, revenge, envy or hatred towards his fellows.' Worship the Lord fearfully.

People :   We will worship and glorify the Lord.

The priest covers the bread and chalice with the veil. He then bows to the altar and the deacon bows to the priest; then they both bow, while the priest continues in a low voice :

We place this bread upon the paten after the manner in which you were placed in the sepulchre and remained there for three days and three nights. Permit my hands to be like the hands of Joseph and Nicodemus who wrapped your body in linen cloths and obtained peace, rest and honour from the Father and from the Son and from the Holy Spirit, now and ever, worlds unceasing. Amen.

The deacon, turning to the West, continues :

Listen to the commandment of our fathers, the Apostles: 'Let no one entertain in his heart feelings of rancour, revenge, envy or hatred towards his fellows.' Worship the Lord fearfully.

People :   We will worship and glorify the Lord.

All present prostrate before the priest who pronounces the Absolution of the Son :

The Lord Jesus Christ, the only-begotten Son, the Word of God the Father, who released us from the bondage of sin through your life-giving and saving sufferings, and who breathed upon your disciples and devout ministers saying, 'Receive the Holy Spirit; whose sins you shall forgive they are forgiven them, and whose sins you shall retain they are retained'; you have granted to your ministers and priests of your church the power to remit sin on earth and to bind or loosen all the bonds of iniquity. We now again earnestly beg of your goodness, O Lover of man, on behalf of these your servants and handmaids, my father and mother, brothers and sisters and also on my own behalf, on me your humble servant, and on behalf of all your people who bow their heads before your holy altar, demonstrate your mercy to us, break and sever all the bonds of sin, whether we have sinned against you knowingly or otherwise, whether by word or deed, because you know man's frailty.

O good Lover of man and Lord of all creation, forgive us our sins, bless, purify and liberate us, absolve all your people *(the names of recently deceased are mentioned)* and grant that we will always have respect for your holy name and do your will.

To you, O Lord and our God and Saviour Jesus Christ, we offer glory and honour, together with your heavenly Father and the Holy Spirit, the life-giver, who is co-equal with you both, now and ever, worlds unceasing. Amen.

There then follows the Litany 'for all conditions and sorts of men' which is read by the deacon or priest; to each petition the people respond: Kyrie Eleison.

THE LITURGY OF THE CATECHUMENS

At the beginning the priest takes five grains of incense, three of which are placed in the censer, while two are retained, one for the reading of the Gospel and one for the moment of consecration. The priest blesses the grains and recites the following prayer:

O Lord my God, I pray and beg you, as you were most pleased with the offering of Abel and the sacrifice of Enoch, Noah and Abraham, as well as with the incense of Aaron, Samuel and Zacharias, so be equally pleased to accept from me this *(pointing to the censer)* sweet and fragrant offering for the forgiveness of my sins and the sins of all your people, for you are full of mercy and to you glory is due together with your only Son and the Holy Spirit now and ever, worlds unceasing.   Amen.

Priest :   Blessed be God, the Father Almighty *(casts incense)*.

People :   Amen.

The assistant priest prays :

And blessed be your only Son, our Lord Jesus Christ, who became man and was born to the virgin Mary for our salvation.

People :   Amen.

Priest :   And blessed be the Holy Spirit and life-giver of us all. May glory and honour be given to the holy Trinity, the Father, Son and Holy Spirit, now and ever, worlds unceasing. Amen. I will offer you incense. All your garments will smell of sweet spices, and may my prayer ascend before you as incense. Again I offer you this *(pointing)* incense for the forgiveness of my sins and the sins of all your people, because your holy name is most sacred and glorious, Father, Son and Holy Spirit, now and ever, worlds unceasing. Amen.

The praises of the angels ascend to you in heaven.

Alleluia to the Father; Alleluia to the Son; Alleluia to the Holy Spirit.

Glory be to the Father; glory be to the Son; glory be to the Holy Spirit.

Let us worship the Father; let us worship the Son; let us worshib the Holy Spirit.

One in Three and Three in One.

The priest recites the Prayer of the Incense :

O Eternal God, the beginning and end, you who sustain all things, understand all things, who existed before all things and who are without end, be with us and remain among us; strengthen our intentions, sanctify our souls and eradicate in us all that is evil. Enable us to make a good sacrifice and pour out your abundant blessings, and so enable us to enter into the holy of holies wherein dwells your presence.

The priest processes around the altar three times preceded by a lighted taper and accompanied by a deacon bearing the Book of the Epistles. While processing, the following prayer and responses are recited :

We pray and beg you, O God, that you remember the one, holy, apostolic Church.

Deacon : Pray for the peace of the church, one, holy, apostolic and orthodox in the Lord.

At each circuit of the altar the people say :

Amen. Kyrie Eleison. Lord, have mercy on us.

Priest : O Lord, remember the honourable and blessed Holy Pope Abba N., and the blessed and honourable Archbishop Abba N.; remember too the Orthodox bishops, priests and deacons.

Deacon : Pray for our Blessed Pope and for all Orthodox bishops, priests and deacons.

Priest : Remember, O Lord, our congregations; never permit them to be separated or removed; build them up into an edifice of prayer, purity and blessing. Grant it, O Lord, to us and to all your servants unto the end of the world.

Deacon : Pray for our congregations and their safekeeping.

Priest : O Lord my God, may your enemies be routed and defeated, and may all that despise your holy and blessed name scatter and run from your power; may all your people be blessed super-abundantly, and may they do your will at all times through your only Son, to whom, with you and the Holy Spirit, be all glory and power now and ever, worlds unceasing. Amen.

Deacon :   Stand up for prayer.

People :   May the Lord have mercy on us.

On ordinary days the priest says :

'You are the golden censer.'

On feast-days the priest and people together recite the following response three times :

O Christ, we worship you, together with your Heavenly Father and the Holy Spirit, the life-giver, because you came to earth and saved us.

While this response is being said the altar is censed three times. The people recite three times :

The Father, the Son and the Holy Spirit, Three in One and One in Three.

During the recitation of the following response by the priest, the icon of the Blessed Virgin is incensed three times :

Grant peace to your dwelling place, the holy church. Pray for us, O virgin Mary, mother of God.

The priest proceeds to the doors facing west, and begins :

You are . . .

The people continue :

the golden censer, which holds the living coals of fire. That man is blessed who receives gifts from your sanctuary. We worship you, O Christ, you who eradicate and remove all sin and error, who were made man and offered yourself as incense and a sacrifice, holy and acceptable. You, O Christ, we worship, together with your Father and the Holy Spirit, the life-giver, because you came and saved us.

The priest then offers incense at the West doors, saying :

Glory and honour be given to the Father, the Son and the Holy Spirit, now and ever, worlds unceasing. Amen.

The priest returns to the sanctuary, where each member of the clergy is incensed. To each cleric he says :

I beg you, my fellow priest, remember me in your prayers.

Each of the priests being incensed makes the following response :

May God receive your sacrifice and be pleased with the fragrance of your incense. May the Lord sustain your priesthood as he accepted the sacrifice of Melchisedec and the incense of both Aaron and Zacharias who were in the Church of the Firstborn.

The priest lays his hand on the head of each deacon, saying :

May you receive the blessing of St Paul.

The priest then stretches out his hand over the people, saying :

The Lord bless you.

The priest then passes around the altar once, and offers incense over it three times, saying :

O Jesus Christ, you accept the penance of the sinful and forgive sins; forgive my sins and the sins of your people. O God, we entreat you to accept the penitence of your servants; distribute your graces upon them for your name's sake, whose children we are, through your only Son, through whom to you and with him and the Holy Spirit be given all glory and power, now and ever, worlds unceasing. Amen.

Deacon :   Stand up for prayer.

People :   Lord, have mercy upon us.

The assistant priest recites the Prayer before the Epistle :

O Lord God, who know all things that are mysteries to man, dispenser of joy to those who proclaim your might, grant that after a similar fashion by which Paul was called, converted and became an apostle and preacher, so may we be favoured with pure understanding and knowledge of your truths and never may we be separated from you. Just as Paul was like you, O Prince of Life, grant that we may be made like him in deed and faith, to praise your holy name, and to glory in the Cross, for to you belong all the power and glory, now and ever, worlds unceasing. Amen.

The deacon recites the following as he proceeds to read the Epistle :

Anyone that does not love our Lord, God and Saviour Jesus Christ and does not believe in his birth of the virgin Mary, and his coming again, let him be anathema; so has Paul written.

The Epistle of Paul is read facing the people; at its conclusion the deacon says :

May the Epistle of Paul serve as a source of purity and be pleasing to the Lord.

The priest goes round to each of the doors and recites the same Doxology as before. He then censes the deacons and people, and returns to the sanctuary where he censes the altar, saying :

O Lord God, who caused the walls of Jericho to collapse through the faith of your servant Josuah, cause the walls of sin of your people to collapse through the efforts of me, your servant.

Priest :   Hail Mary, full of grace.

People :   The Lord is with you.

Priest :   Among women, you are blessed.

People :   And blessed is he, who is born of you.

Priest :   O mother of God, pray and intercede for us.

The altar is then censed again, while the priest says :

O Jesus Christ, you who accept the penance of the sinful and forgive sins, forgive my sins and the sins of your people. O God, we entreat you to accept the penitence of your servants and distribute your graces upon them for your name's sake, whose children we are. Through your only Son, through whom to you, and with him and the Holy Spirit, be given all glory and honour, now and ever, worlds unceasing. Amen.

The deacon re-enters the sanctuary after reading the Pauline Epistle and says :

May the blessing of the Father, and the generosity of the Son and the gifts of the Holy Spirit which came down upon the Apostles in the Upper Room descend upon us and be multiplied in us. Amen.

People :   May the holy Apostle Paul, who was a good messenger and healer of the sick, intercede for us and pray that our souls might be saved by the immensity of God's loving kindness and mercy.

Deacon :   Stand up for prayer.

People :   May the Lord have mercy upon us.

Priest :   Peace be with you all.

People :   And with you.

Priest :   O eternal God, without beginning and without end, who exist in all things, we pray and beg that you be among us today, that we might feel the radiation of your peace and abiding love.

May our hearts be purified and our souls made holy, and grant that whatever sins we have committed may be forgiven, so that we could enter into the holy of holies and present a pure sacrifice and offer a spiritual fragrance that would be counted worthy of your holiness. Through your only Son, our Lord and Saviour Jesus Christ, and through the Holy Spirit.

The subdeacon while going out to read the Catholic Epistle says the following :

The reading from the Epistle of N., disciple and apostle of our Lord Jesus Christ. His prayer and blessing be with us all. Amen.

At the conclusion of the Epistle the subdeacon says :

May this Epistle of the Holy Spirit which comes from the mouth of N., the rock of truth, inspire in us purity and exaltation. God's blessing be with us, forever and ever: Amen.

People : Most holy Trinity, protect this congregation for your disciple's sake; extend to us the benefits of your mercy for your name's sake.

Deacon : Stand up for prayer.

People : May the Lord have mercy upon us.

Priest : Peace be with you all.

People : And with you.

Priest : O Lord our God, who revealed to your holy Apostles the mystery of the Messiah's mission, who gave them the immeasurable gift of grace and sent them out into the world to proclaim the message of your gracious mercy, we beg you to make us worthy heirs to the tradition of the Apostles, so that we might be able to walk in their footsteps and to imitate their fellowship with you. Be pleased to keep and preserve your holy Church *(he blesses himself)* and to bless the faithful *(blesses the people)* and may this wine *(blesses the oblation)* be increased, which has been established by your holy right hand *(blesses the clergy)*. Through our Lord and Saviour Jesus Christ. Amen.

The assistant priest announces the reading from the Acts of the Apostles :

The history of the Acts of the Apostles is a pure stream flowing from the pure spring of Love. May the prayers of the holy Apostles bring us many blessings. Amen.

The assistant priest reads from the Acts of the Apostles. At its conclusion he says :

The Word of God has increased in the holy Church, and

many now believe in our Lord and Saviour Jesus Christ, to whom be glory, now and ever, worlds unceasing. Amen.

People :   Holy, Holy, Holy is the Father Almighty.
Holy, Holy, Holy is the only Son,
   who is the Word of the Father.
Holy, Holy, Holy is the Holy Spirit,
   who knows all things.

THE TRISAGION

The priest while offering incense says the following :

Glory and honour be given to the holy Trinity, the Father, Son and Holy Spirit, now and ever, worlds unceasing. Amen.

The priest says the following prayer while standing before the altar :

O Lord our God, who while accepting the sacrifice of Isaac by his father Abraham provided an alternative sacrifice, namely a ram, deign to accept our sacrifice and the sweet fragrance of this incense, and in return give us your loving-kindness and mercy, so that all the unclean odours of sin might be removed from us, that we become worthy to be ministers before your glorious majesty.

The priest processes around the altar three times and recites the following prayer :

We pray and beg you, O God, that you remember the one, holy and apostolic Church.
   O mother of God, ever a virgin and full of grace, present our prayers to your Son, that he might forgive us our sins. Rejoice, O mother of God, who bore the Light of the world; intercede for us with the Lord, that he might have mercy upon us and forgive us our sins.
   Rejoice then, O mother of God, most holy and pure, and deign to intercede for us with your Son, that he will grant us the forgiveness of our sins.
   O virgin mother of God, most pure and holy Queen of Heaven, be pleased since you bore the Saviour of the world, and be gracious and plead for us, O glorious Mediatrix, before your Son, our Lord and Saviour Jesus Christ.

The priest now goes outside the veil and chants the following versicles alternately with the other clergy, while the second deacon carries the Book of Gospels from the sanctuary, preceded by an acolyte bearing a lighted taper :

℣   Now is the moment of blessing, the occasion when we offer praise to our Saviour Jesus Christ.

℟   Christ who was in Mary's womb is the chosen incense, but is more beautiful and perfumed than all the best and selected incenses. He whom Mary bore came and saved us.

℣   Jesus Christ is like the most fragrant of ointments; let us come and worship him; may we observe his commandments so that he will forgive us our sins.

℟   Michael was given the mission of mercy to bring God's messages to the world, while Gabriel brought a heavenly gift to the blessed virgin Mary.

℣   Understanding was David's gift, while wisdom was given to Solomon, and Samuel was presented with a horn of oil because he anointed the kings.

℟   Peter was given the keys of the Kingdom, while virginity was John's gift and apostleship was given to our father Paul, because he was the light of the church.

℣   Mary is like the most fragrant of ointments, because he that was born of her is more fragrant than all the most beautiful incenses and was made man of her flesh.

℟   In the most pure Mary the Father was exceedingly pleased, and elected her to be the dwelling place for his only Son.

℣   While Moses was given the law, Aaron was given the priesthood and Zacharias was presented with chosen incense.

℟   They prepared a tabernacle according to the Word of God and Aaron offered incense.

℣   The seraphim and cherubim worship and praise him saying: Holy, Holy, Holy is the Lord God, and his honour extends beyond all his creation.

℟   You are the incense, O Saviour, for you came and saved us; have mercy upon us.

The priest says three times in a loud voice :

Holy God, holy mighty God, holy living and immortal God, have mercy upon us.

He continues :

Holy Trinity, pity us.
Holy Trinity, spare us.
Holy Trinity, have mercy upon us.

The priests and other ministers, having left the sanctuary, stand before the veil. The celebrant blesses the assembled clergy, saying :

May glory and honour be given to the holy Trinity, the Father, the Son and the Holy Spirit, now and ever, worlds unceasing. Amen.

Deacon :   Alleluia. Stand up for prayer.

People :   Lord, have mercy upon us.

Priest :   Peace be with you all.

People :   And with you.

The priest recites the Prayer of the Gospel :

O Lord Jesus Christ, who said to your holy disciples and apostles, 'Many prophets and holy men have wished to see the things that you see and have not seen them, and to hear the things that you heard and have not heard them, but you are blessed because of what your eyes have seen and your ears have heard'—make us like them, fitting to hear and to do the word of your holy Gospel, through the intercession of the saints.

Deacon :   Be ready to hear the holy Gospel.

People :   May we be found fit to hear the holy Gospel.

Priest :   O Lord, remember those who have asked us to remember them at this holy time, and be pleased to grant consolation to those who are sick, because you are the source of all life and our eternal hope and deliverance. To you we offer our thanksgiving, now and ever, worlds unceasing. Amen.

The priest then blesses the four extremities of the church, saying :

And may the Lord of us all bless us here ✠ and sanctify us with every spiritual blessing ✠ and may our entry into his holy church ✠ be united with the entry of God's angels, who sing to him with fear and awe ✠ and who offer adoration unceasingly. Amen.

The priest now turns towards the Book of the Gospels and says :

O Lord our God and Saviour, who sent the disciples and apostles to the very ends of the earth to teach and proclaim your message, to heal all illnesses and to reveal the mysteries of the faith which have been hidden from man since the creation of the earth, send us your blessings and enlighten our understanding, and may we be given the gift of final perseverance.

May we be enabled to do and to act in accordance with your commands as set out in the Gospel, and may the fruit of the Gospel be increased in us many times over, that we may obtain forgiveness of our sins, and so be considered worthy to obtain our heavenly reward.

The priest goes around the altar once, a taper carried before him and the Book of the Gospels after him. He blesses the book with the censer, saying :

Blessed be the Lord, the Father Almighty.

Turning towards the people, the assistant priest says :

Give thanks to the Father.

Priest : And blessed be the only Son, our Lord Jesus Christ.

Assistant priest : Give thanks to the Son.

Priest : And blessed be the Holy Spirit, the Comforter.

Assistant priest : Give thanks to the Holy Spirit.

Priest : The Lord be with you all.

People : And with you.

Priest : The holy Gospel which N. preached; the word of the Son of God.

People : May glory be given to you, O Christ, my Lord and my God, always. Praise the Lord and worship at his feet, because he is holy.

Holding the Book of the Gospels before the cross, the assistant priest says :

O God, full of mercy and forgiveness, be pleased to receive our prayers and acts of penitence. Prepare us to hear your holy Gospel, so that in keeping your commandments, we will be living limbs of the Mystical Body.

Remember, O Lord, the catechumens of your people; may they receive the faith and lose all traces of their earlier paganism and learn to fear your almighty power. May they receive the truth, with which they are being instructed, and following this instruction may they be reborn and become worthy vessels of the Holy Spirit, through the love of your only Son, the Lover of man, our Lord and Saviour Jesus Christ, worlds unceasing. Amen.

The priest says the following before the Gospel is announced :

O Lord, we beg you to bless ✠ the reading of the Gospel of N., the disciple and apostle of our Lord Jesus Christ, the only Son of God the Father.

If the Gospel is taken from St John, a special form of blessing is used :

Bless ✠, O Lord, through the Gospel of John the Disciple and Apostle of our Lord Jesus Christ, the Son of the living God; to him be glory continually, world without end. Amen.

The priest, standing between two deacons holding tapers, faces the East and reads the Gospel. On less solemn occasions, a cleric holds a taper before the priest and a deacon holds the Book of the Gospels. At the conclusion of the Gospel the priest kisses the book and says one of the following ejaculations, according to the author of the Gospel just read:

'Heaven and earth and all created matter may disappear, but my word will never be annihilated', said the Lord to his disciples (*St Matthew*).
'He who is willing to hear, let him pay attention' (*St Mark*).
The Lord said, 'It is easier for all creation to disappear than it is for any detail of the Word of God to be changed' (*St Luke*).
'He who believes in the Son of God shall merit everlasting life' (*St John*).

Similarly the people respond according to the author just read:

We believe in the Father, Son and Holy Spirit (*St Matthew*).
The cherubim and seraphim offer glory and praise to God, saying Holy, Holy, Holy, to the Father, Son and Holy Spirit (*St Mark*).
What god is like you, O Lord? You, O Lord, performed miracles, descended into hell, and released those who were waiting your pardon, and to set us free from the chains of sin you came and saved us. Because of this, we offer you praise, saying: You are blessed, O Lord Jesus Christ, because you came and saved us (*St Luke*).
At the beginning of time, the Word already was, and the Word was God. And the Word was made flesh and came to dwell among us and we had sight of his glory, as befitting the only-begotten Son of God, who rose again from the dead. and whose flesh was incorrupt (*St John*).

Deacon :   All catechumens must now leave.

As the priest enters the sanctuary, he recites the Prayer of St Basil:

O Lord our God, who showed your immense love towards us and sent your only Son into the world to rescue us from the ties of sin, we beg you not to spurn us but permit us to approach the Sacrifice without defilement, not relying on our own goodness, but on your abundant mercy. We further pray you, O Lover of man, that this Sacrifice be not for our condemnation, but our salvation and the forgiveness of our sins. May glory and honour be given to your holy name, now and ever, worlds unceasing. Amen.

LITURGY OF THE FAITHFUL

Deacon :   Stand up for prayer.

People :   Lord, have mercy on us.

Priest :   Peace be with you all.

People :   And with you.

Priest :   We once more beg the almighty Lord and Father of our Saviour Jesus Christ to extend his benediction over us and to remember the peace of the Church, holy and apostolic, which extends from one end of the world to the other.

Deacon :   Pray for the peace of the one, holy, apostolic and Orthodox Church.

Priest :   Bless ✠ all the people and all congregations which acknowledge you as the Lord, and grant us that peace which comes from heaven. Grant peace to the sovereign of this realm and to his armies, and may we all live in peace at home and abroad.

    O King of peace, as you have given us everything we possess, grant us peace, and as we call upon your name may our souls be animated by the Holy Spirit and may the death of sin not exercise any hold over us, your servants and your people.

People :   Kyrie Eleison.

Deacon :   Stand up for prayer.

People :   Lord, have mercy on us.

The priest recites the Prayer for the Hierarchy :

    Let us once more beg Almighty God, the Father of the Lord and Saviour Jesus Christ, for the blessed Pope N., that he might be spared to us for many years in peaceful times and successfully fulfil his divine mission. May the Lord our God, who is full of mercy, grant this request.

Deacon :   Pray for our Pope N. and for the blessed Bishop Abba N. and all Orthodox bishops, priests and deacons.

Priest or assistant priest :

    O Lord our God, we pray for our blessed Bishop Abba N. that he might be granted a peaceful life, fulfilling his priesthood which you gave. Similarly we pray for all Orthodox bishops, priests and deacons with their congregations and for the one, holy, catholic and apostolic Church.

    Be pleased, O God, to accept the prayer which he will

make on our behalf and that of all your people. Give him the fullness of the grace of the Holy Spirit, and may the blessing which he will receive be poured out upon us; subdue all his enemies, visible and invisible. Grant him, O God, a long life and a fruitful priesthood, through your only Son, our Lord and Saviour Jesus Christ, to whom with you and the Holy Spirit be all glory given, worlds unceasing. Amen.

Deacon :   Stand up for prayer.

People :   Lord, have mercy upon us.

Priest :   Peace be with you all.

People :   And with you.

Priest :   Let us again beg Almighty God, the Father of our Lord and Saviour Jesus Christ, that he may shower us with his blessing, out of the fullness of his goodness.

Deacon :   Pray for this holy church and the congregation assembled here.

People :   Bless our congregation and keep us peaceful.

Priest :   Grant that your people may be prevented from becoming lazy and spiritually slack, so that they may always be prepared to do your holy and blessed will. Grant us and our children a long life, so that we may build a spiritual edifice of blessing, prayer and purity.

The priest then takes the censer from the assistant priest. He censes the altar three times. Then bowing his head, he proceeds to cense the four corners of the altar, saying :

O Lord, arise and disperse your enemies, and all those that hate your holy and blessed name run away in fear before you.

The priest then blesses the people with the censer and bows three times while continuing the prayer :

And may your people be abundantly blessed, through the grace and compassion of the Lover of man, your only Son, our Lord and Saviour Jesus Christ, to whom, with you and the Holy Spirit, be all glory and honour given, worlds unceasing. Amen.

Deacon :   Let us all say together, in the wisdom of God, the holy prayer of faith.

Priest and people :

We believe in one God, the Father Almighty, maker of heaven and earth, and of all things visible and invisible. And in one Lord Jesus Christ, the only-begotten Son of God, begotten of his Father, before all ages, Light of Light, Very God of Very God, begotten not made, being of one substance with the Father; through whom all things were made; who for us men and for our salvation came down from heaven, and was incarnate by the Holy Spirit of the virgin Mary, and was made man, and was crucified also for us under Pontius Pilate. He suffered and was buried, and the third day he rose again according to the Scriptures, and ascended into heaven, and sits at the right hand of the Father. He will come again in glory to judge the living and the dead, and his reign will have no end. I believe too in the Holy Spirit, the Lord and life-giver, who proceeds from the Father (and the Son), who with the Father and the Son together is worshipped and glorified, who spoke through the prophets. And I believe in one, holy, catholic and apostolic Church. I acknowledge one baptism for the remission of sins, and I look forward to the resurrection of the dead and the life of the world to come. Amen.

At the conclusion of the Creed, the assistant priest takes the covering off the paten, and the priest washes his hands, reciting the Lavabo. He then turns towards the people, sprinkling them with the moisture of his hands :

All those here who are free from impurities may receive the Host, while those who are not pure may not receive at all. I am not to be held responsible for any sacrilege that may be committed against the body and blood of Christ, and if anyone commits a sin in respect of this Holy Sacrament, then the sin will return upon his head and he will be consumed in God's fiery anger.

Deacon : If there is anyone in this church who scoffs at this command and laughs, speaks or behaves evilly while in the church, let him be warned that he is provoking the anger of God, and will draw upon himself a curse and not a blessing, the fire of hell and not the forgiveness of sins.

Priest : O my Lord and God, Creator of order and Giver of peace and love, repel all evil thoughts of revenge and hatred from my mind, and dispel all lusts from my body. Be pleased to number me with your holy servants and those who do your holy will in this life, because you who came down from heaven will give peace to all your people and to those who listen and understand, that they may praise you, for to you belong all praise and glory forever. Amen.

Deacon : Stand up for prayer.

People : Lord, have mercy upon us.

Priest :   Peace be with you all.

People :   And with you.

The priest recites the Prayer of the Salutation :

> O great and eternal God, who created man and abolished death, which came into the world through the envy of Satan, by the incarnation of your living Son, our Lord and our God and Saviour Jesus Christ; you filled the earth with your peace, which originates in heaven, where all the heavenly company glorify you saying: May glory be given to God in heaven and on earth; peace to men who are God's friends.

People :   May glory be given to God in heaven and on earth; peace to all men who are God's friends.

Priest :   O Lord, out of your goodness, eradicate all the corruption in our hearts, and remove all envy, revenge and the hatreds which doom us to death. Make us worthy to greet one another with a devout greeting.

Deacon :   Pray for perfect peace and love; greet one another with a holy salutation.

People :   O Christ, our God, make us worthy to greet one another with a holy greeting.

The priests bow to each other, then the priest-celebrant bows to the deacons, who bow to each other. Then a deacon bows to the people, who bow to each other. The priest-celebrant continues :

> And may we be permitted to partake of your holy, immortal and heavenly gift, without condemnation. Through our Lord and Saviour Jesus Christ, who lives and reigns with you and the Holy Spirit, worlds unceasing. Amen.

THE ANAPHORA OF OUR HOLY FATHERS THE APOSTLES

Priest :   ✚ The Lord be with you all *(blesses himself)*.

People :   And with you.

Priest :   ✚ Lift up your hearts *(the other ministers bless themselves)*.

People :   We have lifted them up to the Lord our God.

Priest :   ✚ Let us give thanks to the Lord our God *(the people bless themselves)*.

People :   It is just and fitting.

Priest :   We give you thanks, O Lord, for your beloved Son, our Lord Jesus Christ, whom you sent to us, and who is your Word, and through whom all things were created by your will.

Deacon :   For the sake of the blessed and holy Pontiff Abba N. and for the blessed Bishop Abba N., while they still offer their prayers and petitions; for the sake of all your saints, Stephen and the first martyrs, who gave their life for the faith; Matthew, Mark, Luke and John the four evangelists; holy Mary, the Mother of God; Simon Peter and Andrew, James, John, Phillip and Bartholomew, Thomas, Matthew, Thadeus and Nathaniel; James the Son of Aphaeus and Mathias, the twelve Apostles and James the Apostle, brother of our Lord, Bishop of Jerusalem; Paul, Timothy, Silas and Barnabas, Titus, Philomen and Clement, the seventy-two disciples, the five hundred brethren, the three hundred and eighteen Orthodox—may the prayers of all of them come to our aid and spiritual assistance.

The priest continues :

And remember the peace of the universal, catholic and apostolic church which was established by Christ through his precious blood. Remember the pope, all patriarchs, metropolitans, bishops, priests, deacons and all Christian people everywhere.

The assistant priest recites the Prayer of Benediction :

Send us the comfort of the Holy Spirit and in mercy and faith may the doors of the holy Church be always open to us, and grant that we will always preserve the faith until our dying day.

O my Lord Jesus Christ, bring relief to those who are suffering and be pleased to grant them health. Protect our families and friends who have gone away, bring them back to their homes, in peace and in health.

Bless the winds of the sky *(the priest blesses in the direction of the sky)*, and the rains and fruits of the earth, in accordance with your will and may joy and happiness be always sustained on the face of the earth *(he blesses in the direction of the ground)*.

Grant peace to our country and to the scholars of your Church; to each and every one of us and to all foreign governments may your peace be extended.

Grant rest, O Lord, to all our fathers, brothers and sisters who have died in the faith.

Bless those, O Lord, who have given gifts of incense *(he blesses the people)*, bread, wine, oil, decorations, books and vessels for the sanctuary, that Christ our God may reward them in the heavenly kingdom.

Bless those who are assembled here with us, begging your mercy; be propitious to them and to those that give alms.

Give comfort to all that are in any way distressed, imprisoned, exiled or in any way held captive; deliver them through your mercy, and be pleased to remember all those people who have asked us to remember them in our prayers, and be pleased to remember me, your sinful servant.

O Lord save your people and bless them ✝. Sustain them and grant them eternal life.

The assistant deacon says the following while the priest faces the people :

Have mercy upon the patriarchs, archbishops, bishops, priests, deacons and all Christian people.

The priest turns and blesses the people twice while the above prayer is being recited. Then he turns back to the altar and continues :

To these and all your people grant peace and be propitious, O God, who sent your Son from heaven to the virgin mother's bosom.

Deacon : You that are sitting down, stand up.

Priest : He who was carried in the womb, and was born, and whose birth was revealed by the Holy Spirit, to you, before whom stand multitudes, the holy angels and archangels and those honourable creatures that have six wings, the seraphim and cherubim . . .

Deacon : Look to the East.

Priest : With two of their wings they cover their faces, while they cover their feet with two of their other wings and with two they fly from one end of the world to the other.

Deacon : Pay attention.

Priest : Receive our humble hallowing, with them that continually hallow and praise you, in this humble manner, saying: Holy, Holy, Holy, perfect Lord of hosts.

A bell is sometimes rung here. The deacon says :

Make your response.

People : Holy, Holy, Holy, perfect Lord of hosts, your glory fills all heaven and earth.

The priest blesses himself, the ministers and people, while saying :

Heaven and earth are full of the immensity of the holiness

of your glory in Christ, who came and was born of the virgin Mary, that he might redeem us and perfect us for you.

People :   Remember us, O Lord, in the same way as you remembered the thief on the cross at your right hand during your holy passion.

The assistant priest places more incense grains in the censer. The priest passes his hands through the smoke, and then passes them over the oblata, having previously censed them, saying :

He stretched out his hands during the passion, suffering to save those that trusted in him; he was delivered to the passion that he might destroy death, sever the bonds of Satan, destroy hell, lead out the saints, and announce his glorious resurrection.

Deacon :   Lift up your hands, O priests of God.

Priest :   In the same night in which they betrayed him, he took bread in his holy hands, which were unspotted and blessed...

The priest raises the bread, continuing :

He looked up to heaven, to you, his Father ✠ gave thanks ✠ blessed ✠ and broke *(the bread is broken in five places but the pieces are not disjoined)* and gave to his disciples and said to them *(he points to the bread and bowing deeply says)* :

TAKE, EAT, THIS IS MY BODY

which is broken for you for the forgiveness of sins.

A bell is rung and the people say :

Amen. Amen. Amen. We believe and confess, we praise you, our Lord and our God. This is true. We believe.

The priest continues :

And likewise ✠ also the cup, giving thanks ✠ he blessed it ✠ and hallowed it and gave it to his disciples and said to them *(the priest points at the chalice, and bows deeply)* :

TAKE, DRINK, THIS IS MY BLOOD

which is shed for you for the remission of sins.

People :   Amen. Amen. Amen. We believe and confess, we praise you, our Lord and our God. This is true. We believe.

The priest now moves the chalice with his right hand in the form of a cross, saying :

As often as you do this, do it in remembrance of me.

People :   We demonstrate your death and holy resurrection, O Lord; we believe your Ascension; we praise, confess and supplicate you, O Lord our God.

THE EPICLESIS

Priest :   Now, O Lord, we remember your death and your resurrection. We acknowledge you and offer to you this *(pointing)* bread and this *(pointing)* cup, giving you thanks for rendering us worthy of the delights in standing before you and ministering to you. We pray and beg the Lord that you would send the Holy Spirit and power upon this *(points)* bread and upon this *(points)* cup. May he make them the body ✠✠✠ and blood ✠✠✠ of our Lord and Saviour Jesus Christ, worlds unceasing.

People :   Amen. Lord, have mercy upon us. Amen. Lord, have mercy upon us. Lord, be kindly disposed towards us.

The priest signs the bread with his thumb intincted with the precious blood :

Give it to all them that take it, and may it be a source of santification and a confirming in the true faith, that they may hallow and praise you and your beloved Son, Jesus Christ, worlds unceasing. Amen.

Deacon :   From the bottom of our hearts we beg the Lord our God that he grant us the good communion of the Holy Spirit.

People :   As it was in the beginning, is now and shall ever be, worlds unceasing. Amen.

The priest divides the bread into thirteen parts, and says alternately with the people, the following versicles and responses.

		1		
	5	9	7	
3	11	13	12	4
	8	10	6	
		2		

Priest :   Grant that we may always be united in your Holy Spirit and that we may be healed by this oblation, so that we may live forever, worlds unceasing. Amen.

People :   Amen. Grant us this request.

Priest :   May the Lord's name be always blessed, and he that comes in the name of the Lord. So be it, so be it, so be it blessed.

The people repeat the words of the priest. The deacon says :

Stand up for prayer.

People :   Lord, have mercy upon us.

Priest :   Peace be to you all.

People :   And with you.

The priest recites the Prayer of Fraction :

Again we beg the Almighty Lord and Father of our Lord Jesus Christ to enable us to partake of this holy Mystery with confidence, to grant us confirmation and not condemnation, and to make all worthy who partake of the holy Mystery of the body and blood of Christ, the almighty Lord our God.

Deacon :   All pray.

The people recite the Lord's prayer. The priest continues :

O Lord, our Almighty God, grant that we may partake effectually of your holy Mystery and that we do not draw condemnation upon us, but may all be blessed in Christ, through whom to you, with him and the Holy Spirit, be glory and dominion, now and ever, worlds unceasing. Amen.

The people recite the following response three times :

According to your mercy, O our God, and not according to our sins.

The assistant priest, subdeacon and people sing or say alternately the following verse three times :

The angelic hosts of the Saviour of the world stand before him and encompass the Saviour of the world, even the body and blood of the Saviour of the world. So let us come before the Saviour of the world. In holy faith let us give thanks to Christ.

The assistant deacon and the subdeacon say the following while entering the sanctuary :

O princes, open up the gates.

Deacon :   You who are standing, bow your heads.

Priest :   O Lord eternal, you who know all things, have regard for your people who now bow their heads before you, and who have subdued their stubborn hearts; from your dwelling place look upon these people, bless them and grant their petitions.

With the strength of your right hand, help and protect them from every evil affliction and be a guardian both to their bodies and souls and increase in them the faith and fear of your holy name. Through your only-begotten Son, through whom . . . Amen.

Deacon :   Worship the Lord fearfully.

People :   We worship before the Lord and glorify him.

The priest recites the Prayer of Penitence of St Basil :

O Lord almighty, it is you who heal our soul, body and spirit, as you revealed through the word of your only Son, our Lord and Saviour Jesus Christ, on the occasion when he spoke to our father Peter: 'You are a rock, and upon this rock I will build my Church and the gates of hell shall not prevail against it, and I will give to you the keys of the kingdom of heaven, and whatever you shall bind on earth, shall be bound in heaven and whatever you shall loose on earth, it shall likewise be loosed in heaven.'

Let all your servants be absolved and released by the operation of the Holy Spirit, through my mouth, your sinful and guilty servant.

O merciful Lover of man, Lord our God, who take away the sins of the world, accept the penitence of your servants; illuminate them with the light of everlasting life and be pleased, O Lord, to forgive them all their sins, for you are the bountiful Lover of man.

O merciful Lord our God, full of forgiveness and slow to anger, forgive me my sins and deliver all your servants from all trespasses and curses. If we have offended the Lord, whether in thought, word or deed, release, remit, pardon and have mercy, for you are God, the Lover of man, O Lord our God.

O Lord absolve us and liberate all your people and be pleased to absolve me, your sinful servant.

The priest takes a corner of the little veil in his right hand and stands half facing the people, with his hand extended towards them and says the following commemoration of the living and the dead. The priest blesses the people three times, facing them and continues :

O Lord, remember the patriarchs, archbishops, bishops, priests and deacons, anagrosts and singers, virgins and monks, widows and orphans, men and women, aged and children, and all Christian peoples that are standing in this holy church; fortify them in the faith of Christ.

The Commemoration of the Dead :

> Remember all our fathers, brothers and sisters that have died in the Orthodox faith; may they rest in the bosoms of Abraham, Isaac and Jacob.
>
> As for us, do not allow us to become victims of your wrath because of our lies, rebellion and sinful acts, but be merciful and preserve us from contact with heretics and gentiles with the risk of defilement.
>
> O Lord, grant us wisdom, strength and the understanding to avoid the temptations of Satan and his minions. Grant O Lord that we will always do your will and that our names will be inscribed in the Book of Life in the heavenly kingdom, with all your saints and martyrs, through Jesus Christ, our Lord, through whom . . . Amen.

Deacon : Let us be attentive.

Holding the host, the priest says :

> Holy things to the holy.

A bell is rung and the people respond :

> One is the holy Father, one is the holy Son and one is the Holy Spirit.

The priest takes the host and blesses the chalice with it :

> ✠ The Lord be with you all.

People : And with you.

The priest lifts up the entire host and says :

> Lord Christ, have mercy upon us.

This is repeated three times in a loud chant, and fifteen times in a low chant. The people repeat the same versicle. The priest takes the host with his hand, dips his finger into the chalice and signs the large portion of the host once on its surface once on its side surface and once on the smaller portions. The deacon says :

> Those of you who are penitent, bow your heads.

The priest faces the people :

> To those who are penitent, have mercy, eradicate their sins, guard, keep and redeem their souls in peace. Forgive their former deeds, unite them with your holy Church, through the grace and compassion of your only-begotten Son, our Lord and Saviour Jesus Christ, through whom, with you and the Holy Spirit, be all glory and honour given, worlds unceasing. Amen.

Deacon :   Stand up for prayer.

People :   Lord, have mercy upon us.

Priest :   Peace be with you all.

People :   And with you.

Pointing at the host, the priest says :

> This is the body of our Lord and Saviour Jesus Christ, which is given for life, salvation and the remission of sins, to them that partake of it in faith. Amen.

People :   Amen.

Pointing at the chalice, the priest says :

> This is the true precious blood of our Lord and Saviour Jesus Christ, which is given for life, salvation and the remission of sins to those who drink it in faith.

People :   Amen.

The priest, pointing, says :

> For this is in truth the body and blood of Emmanuel, our God.

People :   Amen.

Priest :   I believe *(three times)* and I confess until my last breath that this *(pointing)* is the body and blood of our Lord and Saviour Jesus Christ, which he took from the Lady of us all, the holy Mary, and united it with his divinity, without mingling or confusion and without alteration. He truly made a good confession before Pontius Pilate, and gave up his body for us on the holy tree of the Cross, of his own will, for us all.

I believe *(three times)* and confess that his divinity was inseparable from his manhood at all times, and that he gave it up for our sake, for life, salvation and for the remission of our sins, to those that partake of it in faith.

Amen. I believe. I believe. I believe that this is true. Amen.

The priest says inaudibly :

> All glory and all honour and all worship are forever due to the holy Trinity, Father, Son and Holy Spirit, now and ever, worlds unceasing. Amen.

The priest intincts the particle from the chalice and then with this intincted particle he blesses the chalice saying :

> May the Lord be blessed for ever *(he puts the particle in the chalice)*.

The assistant deacon offers water to the priest in which to wash his hands.

O God, behold your Son, the sacrifice that is most pleasing
to you, and through this forgive me, because for my sake
your Son died. Behold the pure blood that was poured out
for my sake upon Golgotha; let it plead for me and receive
my petitions for the sake of it. On account of my sins, your
beloved Son received the spear and nails, and suffered, so
that he would be most pleasing to you. Following this salvation, Satan returned and attacked me with his barbs. Grant
me your mercy, because he who is to judge me is mighty.
The devil seeks my soul and I am in need of protection. I
believe and will persevere in this belief until my dying
breath, that this is the body and blood of Emmanuel, our
true God, which he took of the body of the Lady of us all,
holy Mary.

Before Communion is distributed, all say the following :

O Lord, my house is unworthy of your presence because I
have often provoked you and angered you; by my pollution
of my soul and body, I have done no good at all. But for the
sake of your coming to earth and becoming man for my
salvation, for the sake of your precious Cross and your life-
giving death and resurrection on the third day, I pray and
beg that you would purge me from all guilt and sin and when
I have received your holy Mystery. May it not add to my
condemnation and judgment, but be pleased to have mercy
upon me and in the abundance of your mercy be propitious
towards me and grant me the remission of my sins and life
for my soul. I beg for these graces through the petitions of
the lady Mary, John the Baptist and all your saints and
martyrs, worlds unceasing. Amen.

Before the distribution of Communion, the priest says :

O my Lord Jesus Christ, do not permit this Mystery to increase my guilt, but may it be for the purification of my soul
and body.

*The order of reception of the Elements is : bishops, priests, deacons and other
ministers, then the faithful according to rank; women receive last, while
newly-baptized infants receive immediately after the priests. The priest
gives the particle to himself, and then a particle to the assistant priest, who
delivers the chalice to the priest; then the assistant priest drinks from the
chalice himself. The celebrant distributes the particles to the other priests,
while the assistant priest distributes the chalice. The priest says to each
communicant :*

The Bread of Life which came down from heaven, the body
of Christ.

Communicant :   Amen. In truth, we believe.

When each communicant receives the particle, he places his hand over his mouth, until the sacred species is consumed. The deacon or assistant priest says to each communicant when extending the chalice :

> This is the chalice of life that came down from heaven; this is the blood of Christ.

Communicant :   Amen. In truth, we believe.

When Communion has been distributed, the priest says :

> O my Lord and God, Jesus Christ, I have received your pure body and precious blood, for the forgiveness of my sins and for the removal of all my errors; O Lover of man, let me be full of your praise, for you are to be praised; our salvation is in your name, forever and ever.

The priest, drinking a little water, says :

> I pray you, O Lord, the Good Shepherd, who gave down your life for your sheep, have mercy upon us and pardon us.

Deacon :   Let us now give thanks to the Lord for having participated in his holy things. Grant that what we have received may be as a medicine to our soul's life. We have received his holy body and blood; let us now give thanks to him who rendered us fit to communicate in this precious and holy Mystery.

Priest :   O God my King, I will magnify you and praise your name forever.

People :   Our Father in heaven, do not allow us to be tempted beyond our strength.

Priest :   Every day I will thank you and offer continuous praise to your holy name, forever.

People :   Our Father in heaven, do not allow us to be tempted beyond our strength.

Priest :   I will always praise the Lord, and may all men everywhere give thanks to his holy name forever.

People :   Our Father in heaven, do not allow us to be tempted beyond our strength.

Priest :   Inspiration of souls, Guide of the righteous and Glory of the saints, grant us the grace to always see and listen to you, O Lord. When our souls have been satiated with your grace, may our hearts be so purified that we will understand your greatness, who are so good and the Lover of man.
O God, be gracious to our souls and grant us, your humble servants who have received your body and blood, a pure

and firm intent, for yours is the Kingdom, O Lord, blessed and glorious Father, Son and Holy Spirit, now and ever, worlds unceasing. Amen.

People :   Our Father in heaven, do not allow us to be tempted beyond our strength.

Priest :   Again we beg you, O Lord almighty, Father of the Lord and our Saviour Jesus Christ, that our reception of the holy Mystery be not to our condemnation, but that it may serve as a revivifying force to our souls and bodies, through your only Son, through whom, to you, with him and the Holy Spirit, be all glory and honour rendered, worlds unceasing. Amen.

The purification of the sacred vessels takes place according to the Western method, as in the Missale Romanum. When the Ablutions have been taken, the vessels are covered with a veil and are taken to the sacristy. The priest continues :

Your holy, incorruptible Mystery, which you have given us, has been perfectly completed. Make us heirs of the heavenly Kingdom and protect us now and at all times, because you are a glorious king and ruler of all men. To you, our Lord and Saviour Jesus Christ, we offer thanksgiving and honour, together with your Father and the life-giving Holy Spirit, now and forever, worlds unceasing. Amen.

Deacon :   We beg, Almighty God, to inscribe our names in the Book of Life and to bring us to dwell with the saints and martyrs in his heavenly Kingdom. For our absent fathers, brothers and sisters, we beg that they may be delivered from the attractions of the world, and that they may be granted a good nature, love, faith and hope, through the merits of the body and blood of the Son of God. Amen. So be it, so be it.

The priest recites the Prayer of the Imposition of the Hand :

Lord eternal, Life unquenchable, look upon your servants and sow in their hearts the respect and fear of your holy name, and give them to bear fruit to that which in your name has been given to them, even your body and blood. May your hand rest upon those who have bowed their heads before you, your people, men and women, adults and children, virgins and monks, widows and orphans. Also protect us here in this church, and aid us with the strength of your archangels against every evil deed and unite us with Christ our Lord and Saviour; through whom, to you . . . Amen.

The assistant priest prays:

Preserve them in the right faith, in honour all their life long, and embue them with love and peace which is above all understanding and above all wisdom.

By the holy Mother of God's intercession and supplication on our behalf, by the four luminaries, Michael, Gabriel, Raphael and Uriel, and by the four incorporeal creatures and the twenty-four elders and our holy fathers of exalted memory, the chief of the Fathers, Isaac, Jacob and St John the Baptist, and by the one hundred and forty-four thousand. And by our fathers, the Apostles, the seventy-two disciples and St Mark the Evangelist, Apostle and Martyr, the three hundred and eighteen Orthodox who were at Nicaea, the one hundred and fifty bishops in the Province of Constantinople, the two hundred Ephesians, the holy children, St Stephen, the head of the deacons and the first martyr, St George and St Theodore the Illuminator, St Mercury, St Menmas, St Mermehnam, St Kirkos and St Theodore, St Manadelewos and St Claudius, St Philotheus, St Basilide, St Victor, St Abli, St Esdenos, the holy Abba Nob, virgin and singular martyr Eleazor; the warriors and all martyrs; the righteous Father Antony and our holy father, the three Macarii and our Father Abba John Hedir, and our Father Abba Besoi and our Father Abba John Kama and the righteous Abba Bul and our Father Abba Barsuma and our Father Abba Sinoda and our Father St Arsenius and St Theodore, son of our Father Abba Pachomius and our Father Abba Agton and our Father Abba Kiros, and our Fathers Abba Sanael and Gedmawi together with our Roman Fathers Maximus, Demetrius, the strong and holy Abba Moses the black, the forty-nine martyrs and all those who wear the Cross, righteous warriors, martyrs, the elect, the angels and the angel of this blessed day. We seek their intercession and the grace of their assistance, worlds unceasing. Amen.

O Jesus Christ, King of Peace, give us your peace and forgive us our sins and make us worthy to go out and return to our homes in peace.

Deacon : Bow your heads before the Lord our God, so that by the hand of his servant the priest he may bless us.

People : Amen. The Lord bless and pardon us.

Priest : ✚ O Lord save your people and bless your inheritance. ✚✚✚ Sustain them and establish them. Maintain your Church which has been established by the precious blood of your Son, our Lord and Saviour Jesus Christ, to be a con-

gregation for kings and princes and to be for a pure genera-
tion and people.

The priest stands at the door of the sanctuary and says the following prayer :

May you who have come and who will go away and who have
prayed in this holy church and who have fed upon the blessed
body and blood of our Lord and Saviour Jesus Christ, which
is a medicine for the soul, be crucified in his body, the body
divine, and in his blood, the blood of the law. May this
oblation of Jesus Christ, the Son of God, begotten of Mary,
immaculate in virginity, preserve us in peace forever and
ever.

*The priest blesses the people with his finger touching their foreheads ; in the
event of large congregations this is obviously impossible and a more general
Blessing is used. The priest blesses the other priests by taking the hands of
each and saying :*

The power of our Father Peter is with you.

They answer : May God appoint you to a place in his Kingdom.

To the deacons the priest says :

May the most high God bless you and enlighten you.

To the faithful he says :

May the most high God bless you and be pleased with you.

Priest : The Lord be with you all.

People : And with you.
 May God bless us, his servants. May we receive remission
of our sins through the reception of the body and blood of
Christ, our Lord. May the Holy Spirit enable us to conquer
all the influence of the devil. We all look for the blessing
from your merciful hands, and may we be united in our
performance of charitable works.
 May God be blessed in giving us his precious body and
blood and may we find life through the power of the Cross of
Christ.
 To you, O God, we give thanks for all the graces we have
received through the Holy Spirit.

Deacon : Depart in peace.

*Except following a solemn celebration of the liturgy, 'holy bread', i.e. the
loaves brought for the Offertory but not used, are now distributed. The
assistant priest recites this prayer during the distribution :*

O our Lord and Creator, you who fulfil our every need and
provide us with food, may we who fear your holy name

receive your blessings. Extend your right hand and bless ✠ this bread in my hand; may your blessing and goodness descend upon it, so that through it our souls may obtain salvation and our bodies nutrition. The food which you have given us for thanksgiving is yours; may we, O holy Trinity, Father, Son and Holy Spirit, always praise your Kingdom.

O Lord, bless this bread and him who distributes it as well as him who receives it and him who ministers it in your fear. Glory be to the Father and to the Son and to the Holy Spirit, now and forever. Amen.

The Syrian Liturgy

INTRODUCTION

1. *History*

The origins of the Syrian rite are a little obscure. According to some sources its origin is to be found in the legend of Abgar and his correspondence with Christ, the whole of which is of course apocryphal, and is to the effect that St Thomas on his way to India established Christianity in Mesopotamia, Assyria and Persia, having left the apostles Addai and Maris in charge, and it is to these apostles that the origin of the East Syrian and Nestorian rites are attributed. According to Syriac tradition, Addai was one of the seventy-two disciples mentioned in Luke 10:1. The name is philologically the same as Thaddaeus, with whom Eusebius in fact identified him.

The Syriac Liturgy of St James, the brother of the Lord, was the rite of Antioch and is thought by most scholars, especially Don Mercier, to date from the fourth or fifth century. Its connection with the first bishop of Jerusalem is of course quite nominal.

Following upon the Council of Chalcedon, which gave rise to the Monophysite Schism, the patriarchate of Antioch vacillated between the orthodox Catholics and the Monophysites, until the Emperor Justinian I imprisoned all who openly professed Monophysitism.

The Empress Theodora had been instrumental in securing Pope Vigilius's election on the understanding that he would obtain concessions in favour of Monophysitism. It further transpired through the intrigues of the Empress that two monks were clandestinely consecrated while in prison. It can be said that the Syrian Church as a schismatic entity dates from this consecration by Theodosius, the imprisoned Monophysite patriarch of Alexandria; the new prelates were Theodore and James (Jacob) Baradeus. The name Baradeus is said to have originated from the tattered robe (*bárdá 'thân*) in which the prelate is reputed to have travelled while presenting himself as the driving force of Syrian Monophysitism; he died in 578.

Syrian Christians separated into two principal divisions, the orthodox Catholics (Melkites) and the Monophysites or Jacobites, so named after their leader.

It was in the year 629, during the patriarchate of Gregory, that the caliphs of Babylon began to spread their influence throughout Syria and Antioch. Arabic was imposed upon the people and Greek was forbidden, even in the celebration of the liturgy.

The Jacobites successfully carried out missionary incursions into Persia, and this was of course met by very strong opposition on the part of the Nestorians; however it was not long before the Jacobites established a primate in Persia, probably in 630. When the Arabs arrived in 633, the Jacobites, partly on account of their hostility to the Greeks and partly by reason of their usefulness to the conquerors, received preferential treatment. But such a state of affairs was short-lived; the Arabs meted out patronage and martyrdom alternately and many apostatized to Islam, a move which decimated their numbers.

Despite the external troubles which the Church was undergoing, it was also a period of great intellectual and scholarly accomplishment, as seen, for example, by the work of Barhebraeus and James of Edessa.

Hopes for the return of the Jacobites to unity at the Council of Florence in 1439 came to nothing. The decree *Cantate Domino* in 1441, which was aimed at enlightening the dissident Syrians, certainly failed to accomplish its purpose. Three years later the patriarch Ignatius V sent Abdallah, the archbishop of Edessa, as a delegate to Rome, where agreement was arrived at on the three main disputed matters: the procession of the Holy Spirit, the two natures of our Lord, and the two wills of our Lord. In spite of the Decree of Union that resulted from this agreement, the final result was negative.

In 1583 Pope Gregory dispatched a legate to Aleppo; he was entrusted with the task of laying the foundation for the future success of the Franciscan and Jesuit missions which subsequently arrived in 1626.

The seventeenth century was more propitious for the cause of Catholicism in Syria than ever before. In fact the Jacobites seemed to indicate their earnestness for union with Rome. Eventually, in 1656, a Catholic, Andrew Akijian, was elected to the vacant see of Aleppo, and was consecrated by the Maronite patriarch. Subsequently Akijian became the Syrian patriarch.

Unfortunately the Jacobites, who continued to be dissappointed with the 'unity' arrangements, embarked on a campaign of violence, which culminated in the death of the Catholic Syrian leader Peter and some of his clergy. This was accompanied by very stern and severe reprisals against the Catholics, which almost destroyed their cohesive loyalty.

The election of a recent but comparatively secret convert, Mar Michael Jarweh, to succeed the Jacobite patriarch of Antioch, was of course violently opposed by the militant dissidents. They succeeded in having Jarweh imprisoned with the connivance of the Turkish authorities. He eventually escaped from prison, allegedly with the aid of a princess, and made his way to Lebanon; it was from Sharfeh that he governed his people until his death in 1801.

In 1830 the patriarch returned to Aleppo, on the assurance given by

Group of church members in Singapore (Dissident Syrian)

His Holiness Ignatius Yacob III, Syrian Orthodox Patriarch of Antioch and all the East

the Turks that the Catholics would be recognized as a body distinct from the Jacobites. In the years that followed, many Jacobite clergy, including bishops, embraced the Catholic faith, but renewed persecution by the Moslems and the militant Jacobites compelled the patriarch to move from Aleppo to Mardin.

The commencement of World War I saw lay Jacobites able to exercise an active role in the administration of the church, but after brutal attacks and murders by the Turks, the remnant fled into exile.

The events which culminated in the murder of Mar Flavian and some of his clergy in 1915 finally persuaded the Catholic patriarch, Ephrem II Rahmani, a great liturgical scholar, to leave Mardin and to take up residence at Beirut, where the patriarchal residence has remained ever since.

The present Jacobite patriarch lives at Homs, Syria, and is advised by a council, which includes two metropolitans who are without dioceses. This council undertakes most administrative work, such as appointments, ordinations and consecrations.

Upon the Jacobite patriarch's election, the name Ignatius is always added to his own. This is done in memory of the bishop of Antioch who was martyred at Rome in 107. The Syrians believe that this same Ignatius taught the orthodox Christians to bless themselves with the three touching fingers of the right hand, in honour of the indivisible Trinity.

Usually the 'Mafrian and Catholicos of the East', who is the patriarch's vicar-general in Jerusalem, is elected to the patriarchate by the other bishops, who must always consult the faithful.

The bishops are always drawn from the body of monks, but, sad to say, the state of monasticism among the Jacobites is very meagre and of a poor standard. The monks observe the Rule of St Antony and reputedly they practise a most austere and ascetic life.

The Catholic Syrian patriarch of Antioch is elected by the bishops of the church, but the choice must be ratified by Rome. As among the Jacobites, the patriarch, upon election, also assumes the name of Ignatius in addition to his own name.

When a see becomes vacant, the bishop is chosen by the patriarch in consultation with the synod of bishops who in turn consult with the diocesan clergy; again this election must be approved by the Holy See.

II.   *Church buildings*

In most Syrian churches there are three altars in a row, the centre one being surmounted by a canopy; on its gradine there are usually two candles and a crucifix. The other altars are frequently used as credence tables. Syrian altars are approached by three steps, while the Malabar

The church of
Carasoche in Trap
(Catholic.Syrian)

His Beatitude Mar
Ignatius Antony
Hayek,
Patriarch of Antioch
(Catholic Syrian)

Jacobites seem to employ only one. A canopy curtain is drawn around the altar during certain parts of the liturgy or when the altar is not in use. The top of the altar is either wood or stone, covered by a cloth with a silk or linen cloth beneath. The altar stone or *tablith* is consecrated with chrism by the bishop on Holy Thursday or on any Thursday from Easter to the Ascension. The Jacobites speak of the Trinity as having consecrated the stone, which is covered by a cloth, folded in four and often embroidered. Among the Syrians, each tablith bears the name of the consecrating bishop and the date on which the stone was consecrated.

Syrian altars stand away from the wall, in order to allow processions to pass around it. The furniture of the sanctuary is completed by the presence of two episcopal thrones, both on the north side, one facing west, the other south, for use during the liturgy.

One interesting feature of Syrian churches is the sparseness of their interior decorations and the absence of pictures. In some Catholic Syrian churches, statues have replaced the few icons the church may have felt impelled to display.

III.   *Altar vessels*

There is usually quite an assortment of liturgical objects in use. The paten (*pinko*) is rather like a round dish about seven inches in diameter and approximately one inch deep, while the chalice is of the common Western design. Both chalice and paten are fitted with metal lids or stiffened cloths.

The altar bread used is round, thick and leavened, and marked with twelve crosses. The bread to be used in the liturgy is most carefully prepared and baked. The reserved Host, upon which a few drops of the Precious Blood have been sprinkled, has to be renewed daily if possible.

The star (*kaukbo*) can be collapsed and folded when not in use and is designed to prevent the veils from touching the Elements. The spoon (*tarwodho*) is used to communicate those in Holy Orders and the sponge (*espugo*) is used to cleanse the chalice. The origin of the sponge is undoubtedly Eastern and the use made by the Malabar Jacobites of a piece of silk is determined by their distance from the sea. The spoon rests on a cushion (*gomuro*), which can also be used to wipe the fingers and mouth as well as to purify the paten after use. In Jacobite churches one often finds a metal vase upon the altar, which is used to purify the fingers, the contents of which are usually poured down a piscina. In addition there are three veils used for covering the vessels, one for the paten, one for the chalice, known as the *huppayo*, and one to cover both chalice and paten and which is called the *annaphuro*.

Syrian Orthodox priest in his liturgical
vestments (Revd Fr T. J. Abraham).
Vestments worn by Dissident and Catholic alike.

The fans or *Marwah'tho* are most frequently used in this rite and consist of metal discs modelled in the form of a seraph's face and wings; bells are usually attached to it and the whole is connected to a staff. When not in use, fans are placed behind the altar, against the East wall.

Cymbals, together with the *noqusho* or tongueless bronze cup with handle, are struck by a metal rod at solemn parts of the liturgy, for example, at the Sanctus, Consecration, the Elevation and the Blessing of the people.

The thurible used is of Western shape, but with shorter chains and has bells attached. An interesting feature of the thurible's use is that it is always swung its entire length, unlike the standard practice in the West.

iv. *Language and Anaphoras*

The Liturgy of St James was first found at Antioch and was used at Jerusalem and in Arabia, Syria, Armenia, the Slavonic countries, Greece and Ethiopia. The language used is Syriac, a dialect of Aramaic with Western pronunciation and characters.

Though the Catholic Syrians use a liturgy of the Pre-Sanctified during Lent, the Jacobites do not follow suit. The Liturgy of St James was translated from the Greek original into Syriac and it is in this language that the Jacobites celebrate their liturgy. Most Jacobites are familiar with Arabic and on occasions the creed and lessons are recited in this language.

There are some sixty-four known Syrian Anaphoras in all, but only seven are ever included in any Catholic publication. Anaphoras often employed by the Syrians include that of 'St John the Evangelist', 'The Twelve Apostles', 'St Mark the Evangelist' and 'St Eustace of Antioch'.

v. *Vestments*

The alb (*kuthino*) is a long flowing tunic which may be of any colour and can be composed of cotton, linen or silk.

The cincture (*zunnoro*) is not worn by clerics in the lower orders; the priest wears an embroidered belt secured around his waist by two clasps.

The stole (*uroro*) is a broad strip of material with an aperture for the head; usually it is most elaborately adorned and covered with crosses. The priest wears the stole after the Byzantine fashion, while the deacon wears a stole on his left shoulder, from whence it falls to the ground, before and behind, rather like the Russians. An archdeacon wears the stole in a Latin fashion, but he has it secured on the right-hand side.

The subdeacon wears a stole on the left shoulder with the hanging part behind, being brought around under the right arm and thrown back over the left shoulder. The readers wear the stole around the waist, with the two ends crossed and then brought over the breast and tucked into the part that forms the belt.

Cuffs (*zendo*) are used to confine the sleeves of the alb, but should not be considered as modifications of the Latin maniple.

The vestment (*phaino*) is the old *phelonion* or *paenula*, but it is divided up the front and fastened together by a loop, button or clasp. In general appearance it is best described as being cope-like.

Syrian bishops wear a *masnaphto* or hood. It is received during the ceremony of consecration to the episcopacy. During the celebration of the liturgy it covers the head, except during the Gospel, Consecration and post-consecration prayers, when it is worn around the neck. When a mitre is worn, the masnaphto is folded across the shoulders.

The Western-shaped mitre is used by the Catholic Syrian bishops alone, but both Catholic and Jacobite bishops wear the *eskhimo* or *schema*, which is like a small hood; its style varies considerably. The schema of the Catholic bishops is gold in colour and white for monks; it has no ornamentation except for a small cross over the forehead. The Jacobite schema is more elaborate, and is characterized by two white strips, between which is a panel covered by many white crosses.

In outdoor dress, the Jacobite Syrian bishops wear the schema covered with an episcopal turban, while the Catholic bishops wear a *kalemaukion*. The Jacobite secular priests wear a distinctive black cassock or *aba*, together with a wide-sleeved open gown, as well as a black turban or *kawok*.

During the liturgy, Jacobite priests wear a black head-covering or *tarbush*, which is ornamented with seven white crosses. This is removed at the Gospel and from the Preface until the Ablutions.

Syrian bishops bless the faithful with a small hand cross, the *shushepo*, to which is attached a veil and which is carried in the right hand. When not in use the bishop keeps it in a small pocket.

VI. *Calendar*

The Gregorian reckoning is in use and the ecclesiastical year begins on the Sunday nearest 31 October. The use of the Gregorian reckoning has been approved by the Jacobites, except for determining the occurrence of Easter and its associated feasts.

The Syrian church seasons are Advent, Preparation for Lent, Lent, paschal time, the time after Pentecost and the time after the Holy Cross.

In the Syrian calendar there are some beautiful commemorations; for example, each Sunday in Lent commemorates one of the great miracles of our Lord. 'Golden Friday' (the Friday after Pentecost) is so called because it reminds us of the miraculous healing at the Gate Beautiful. Other unusual feasts include the feast of the Praises of Our Lady, celebrated on 26 December and the feast of the Praise of St John the Forerunner, celebrated on 7 January.

The fasts that are observed are often quite protracted from a Western viewpoint; for example, the Assumption fast lasts from 8 to 14 August. In connection with the feast of the Assumption, it should be noted that the Syrians have an unusual custom of gathering in the cemeteries on the feast day; they sit upon the graves of their dead and eat blessed grapes. Whatever remains of this repast, they give to the poor of the locality.

Other fasts include those of the Apostle, which lasts from 16 to 28 June and the Christmas fast from 16 to 24 December. All these fasts are most rigorously and piously observed.

VII.   Sacraments

1) *Baptism*—The Syrians prefer to have their children baptized on the day of the Theophany (Epiphany) or on the Vigil of St John the Baptist.

Before each baptism the water is specially prepared. Following certain prayers of exorcism, the child is anointed three times on the forehead with oil. Then, naked, the child is made to sit in the font and water is poured over its head three times, while the following is said: 'The servant of God N. is baptized in the Name of the Father and of the Son and of the Holy Spirit unto everlasting life.' In true Eastern form, the priest immediately proceeds to administer confirmation.

2) *Confirmation*—This sacrament is administered by the priest, who anoints the forehead, eyelids, nostrils, lips, ears, hands, chest, back and feet with the chrism which was blessed by the patriarch on Maundy Thursday. The words of ministration are: 'N. is sealed unto everlasting life in the Name of the Father and of the Son and of the Holy Spirit with holy chrism, the sweet perfume of the Anointed of God, the sign and seal of true faith and of the accomplishment of the gifts of the Holy Spirit.'

3) *Penance*—This sacrament is given with the Western formula, though there are different formulas appropriate to different sins. Among the Jacobites, in company with other dissident and schismatic churches, this sacrament is often administered rather vaguely and infrequently.

4) *The Eucharist*—For the reception of the sacrament the communicant usually stands, while the celebrant places a Particle, that has been intincted, into the communicant's mouth. The deacon and subdeacon receive by means of the spoon from the chalice.

The Sacrament of the Holy Matrimony, being performed by
His Grace Abraham Mar Clemens, Metropolitan of the Knanaya Diocese
(Dissident Syrian)

It may be of interest to note that among the Jacobites the liturgy is celebrated only on Sundays, except on Holy Thursday when separate liturgies are celebrated at different altars. The Jacobites have no tradition of concelebration.

5) *Anointing*—Among the Catholic Syrians this sacrament combines Western and Eastern usages, the oil of the sick having been blessed by the bishop on Holy Thursday. Among the Jacobites, the sacrament is administered by one priest and it is he who blesses the oil. The Jacobites give this sacrament not only to those who are ill, but even to those who are certainly dead.

6) *Holy Orders*—The orders of the Syrian rite are singer, reader, subdeacon, deacon, priest and bishop. All these orders are conferred during the celebration of the liturgy, accompanied by the laying on of hands and the prorection of instruments but unaccompanied by anointing. Furthermore there is no concelebration at the ordination and consecration Masses for new priests or bishops.

7) *Marriage*—There is no difference between the Jacobites and the Catholics in the administration of this sacrament. Basically it consists of two parts, the blessing of the ring and the crowning. A ring is given to both bride and bridegroom and both are crowned with a wreath, which they retain until the end of the ceremony. In general, the Syrian administration of this sacrament is quite similar to the Byzantine tradition.

VIII.   *Sources of liturgical texts*

Brightman, F. E., *Liturgies Eastern and Western*, Oxford, 1896.
Codrington, H. W., *Studies of the Syrian Liturgies*, London, 1953.
Prince Maximillian of Saxony, *Missa Syriaca-Antiochena*, 1908.
Petit Manuel de la Messe Syrienne, Paris 1923.
Petit Paroissien des Liturgies Orientales, Libya, 1941.

SYRIAN LITURGY

The priest in outdoor dress comes to the foot of the altar and with crossed arms recites the preparatory prayers:

> Glory be to the Father, and to the Son and to the Holy Spirit, and may you be merciful and gracious to us poor and miserable sinners, at all times.
>
> Grant us, O God, tu stand before you in fear and reverence, so that we might serve you as our Creator, to whom worship is due from us all, Father, Son and Holy Spirit, now and forever. Amen.

Psalm 51, Miserere, *is recited by the priest standing before the sanctuary gates. Jacobite Syrians usually squat on their haunches during the recitation of this psalm. At its conclusion, the priest enters the sanctuary, ascends the altar, kisses it and then lights the candles, first on the right and then on the left. Priest:*

> And to you, O God, belongs all glory now and at all times forever. Amen.

The priest addresses the congregation from the plano of the altar:

> Grant us pardon, O Lord.

People: May I be remembered in the Sacrifice.

Priest: Brethren, pray for me.

The priest now ascends the altar, saying the following prayer:

> I will go to the altar of God, to God who gladdens my youthful heart. *(He now bows before the altar saying:)* I have entered your house, O Lord, and have worshipped in your sanctuary, O King of heaven; forgive me all my sins. *(He now kisses the altar three times and then kisses the side of the altar saying:)* Ratify, O God, what we are about to celebrate. My God, I confess and glorify you.

It may be of interest to note that the position of the Prothesis and Vesting is not universally the same. In some locations the Prothesis precedes the Vesting. At the Vesting, the priest takes off his outer ordinary clothes, while saying the following prayer:

> Remove these clothes with which Satan has clothed me, by releasing me from the dominion of my evil thoughts and clothing me in the robes that are fitting for the service of your glory and the praise of your holy Name.

Putting on the cuthino or alb :

> O Lord clothe me in incorruption and strengthen me with the strength of the Holy Spirit.

Putting on the uroro or stole :

> O mighty God, may I be armed with the sword of the Spirit, according to the measure of your renown and worship.

Putting on the left zendo or cuff :

> May my limbs be doers of goodness, O Lord, and fitting instruments of righteousness; make us fitting for the service of your glory and the praise of your holy Name forever. Amen. O God, teach me to fight the good fight and may my strength be like that of tempered steel.

Putting on the right zendo or cuff :

> Make my limbs the fitting instruments of your righteousness and suited to the service of your glory and the praise of your holy Name forever. Amen. Your right hand will support me and your loving correction will improve me and not permit me to lose my foothold.

Putting on the phaino or vestment and signing it with three crosses :

> May your priests be clothed with goodness and your saints with joyfulness. For your servant David's sake, do not forsake us.

The priest now commences the preparation of the altar. He spreads the corporal, uncovers and arranges the vessels; the sponge, spoon and paten are put on the left-hand side, while the chalice is placed to the right. The candles, if not already lit at this point in the liturgy, are lit during the recitation of the following prayers. Priest, lighting those on the right-hand side :

> In your light may we see the Light, O Christ, who are the true light which illuminates every creature, and endows us with understanding.

Lighting those on the left-hand side :

> O you who are so sacred and holy, the source of all divine illumination, keep at bay all evil passions and hateful thoughts, and grant that with pure intentions we might perform the works of goodness.

THE PROTHESIS

Taking the cake of bread in both hands, the priest recites the following :

Like a lamb he was led to the slaughterers, and was as silent as a sheep before the shearer, and throughout his humiliation, he did not say a word.

The breads are arranged decently on the paten; if there are many they are arranged on the paten's edge, crosswise. The priest now covers the paten with both hands saying:

First begotten of the heavenly Father, receive this first-born from the hands of your worthless servant. Bless and consecrate the sanctuary which you have prepared for these first-fruits. The Lord will reign always.

Wine and water are then mixed together.

Our Lord Jesus Christ was crucified between two thieves in Jerusalem and his side was pierced with the lance, and from it blood and water flowed for the redemption of the whole world, and he who saw this, recorded it and we know that his account is true.

The priest slightly raises the chalice and says:

What gift will I give to the Lord in return for all that he has done for me (*Ps 16:13–14*).

The Prothesis ends with the covering of the chalice and paten with the small veils. Priest, covering the paten:

The Lord reigned in his magnificence.

Covering the chalice:

The strength of the Lord secured the earth that it should not falter.

Deacon : Let us stand. May the Lord have mercy upon us.

The priest now descends from the altar and recites the following prayers known as the Proem, Sedro, Quolo and Etro of Penitence.

Proem : Praise is due to him whom every creature, saint and angel, adore and minister.

Sedro : O God, gentle and kind and the humble lover of mankind, you who are more pleased with heartfelt contrition than with the sacrifice of burnt offerings, and prefer the truly humble spirit to the odour and sacrifice of bullocks and lambs; be pleased, O God, to receive our spiritual sacrifice at this moment and consider us worthy to present to you our souls as a living sacrifice, holy and acceptable. May our contrite and humble spirits be as spiritual sacrifices on your exalted altar so that we may appear as a changed and resplendent body of faithful and that in our new glorious strength we may be considered worthy to say: Glory be to the Father, and to the Son and to the Holy Spirit, now and forever. Amen.

Quolo :   O Lord I knock at your holy door and ask for mercy. For years I have been a sinner and now I seek the opportunity to confess my sins and to live forever in your grace and favour. To whom should we address our appeals if your mercy will not grant us pardon and forgiveness, O King of infinite glory?

The Gloria is recited as before in the Sedro. The priest then continues the Quolo :

O Father, Son and Holy Spirit, be a place of security and safety from the assaults of the Devil, who is constantly warring against us; in your mercy may we find protection when the good and bad are separated at the end of the world. May our prayers act as keys to open the heavenly gates and may the holy archangels sing and endorse our humble petitions for mercy.

Deacon :   Have mercy upon us, O Lord, and assist us.

Etro :   May you, O Lord, find the fragrance of our prayers pleasing and through the perfume of our incense may your creatures be reconciled to you, for your mercies' sake, now and until the world's end.

Examen :   (*silence*)

Priest :   I have sinned against you; you who have pity for a sinner, receive my plea for pardon and forgive me my failings. O universal Lord, have mercy on me.

People :   Kyrie Eleison, Kyrie Eleison, Kyrie Eleison.

Priest :   O our Lord, have mercy upon us.
O our Lord, be propitious and have mercy upon us.
O our Lord, hear us and be merciful.
Glory be to you, O Lord,
Glory be to you, O Lord,
Glory be to you, our eternal hope.
Pater Noster.
May we be considered worthy to offer sacrifices of praise to you, O Lord, together with all our thoughts, words and deeds so that we may appear before you spotlessly pure for the rest of our days. Glory be to the Father and to the Son and to the Holy Spirit, always. Amen.

The Sacrifice of Aaron or Kurbono

Priest :   Glory be to the Father and to the Son and to the Holy Spirit; and may we weak and sinful creatures receive mercy and grace always. May we be considered worthy, after we have been purified from all evil influence, to enter the sanctuary

and to stand before your holy altar, there to present to you
in faith, our spiritual sacrifice, Father, Son and Holy Spirit,
now and forever. Amen.

*If a bishop is present, he is censed at the throne by the deacon. Meanwhile
the priest bows down and says the following secretly:*

To you, O God, who forgive the guilty their sins, I stretch
out my hands and beg of you such forgiveness despite my
unworthiness. I beg you to preserve my mind from the
distractions of the Devil, my eyes from the temptations of
the lustful, my ears that they pay no attention to vanities,
my hands that they may always do your service and that I
may constantly strive for your greater glory. From you may
I receive the gift of your divine Mysteries, O Christ our
Lord. Amen.

The priest then kisses the step of the altar, ascends the steps and says:

Stamen Kalos!

People: Kyrie Eleison.

*The priest then uncovers the gifts and places the veil of the paten towards
the south (right side) and the veil of the chalice towards the north. Then,
crossing his hands, the right over the left, he takes the paten in his right
hand and the chalice in his left, and holds them in this position while he
recites the offertory prayer. Over the paten:*

The Lord reigns as king, robed in majesty; the Lord has
royalty as a robe and girdle. He it was who created the earth
and made it immovable. Your throne stood firm before all
time; forever and for all times, you are! The rivers in flood
echo loudly and in their eddying, roar majestically. The
sea also rages. But above all this power, the Lord reigns
supremely magnificent. How faithful, O Lord are your
promises. Holy is your house and is so until the end of
time (*Ps 93, Syriac*).

Over the chalice:

O pure and spotless Lamb who offered his Father an offering
as an atonement and redemption for the world, be pleased
to allow us to offer ourselves to you as a living and pleasing
sacrifice, like the sacrifice which you offered for us, O
Christ our God. Amen.

THE OFFERTORY PRAYER

(THE MEMORIAL OF OUR LORD)

Priest: We commemorate our Lord, God and Saviour Jesus Christ and all his dispensations on our behalf, in particular that of his annunciation by the archangel, his birth in the flesh, his baptism in the river Jordan, his saving passion, his elevation on the cross, his life-giving death, his honourable burial, his glorious resurrection, his ascension into heaven and his installation at the right hand of almighty God.

We make further commemoration at this Eucharist in the first place of our father Adam and our mother Eve, Mary the mother of God, the apostles, preachers, evangelists, martyrs, confessors, just men, priests and holy fathers, true pastors, orthodox doctors, hermits, monks, those who pray together with us and those who have pleased you from the time of Adam and Eve until now.

We also commemorate our fathers and brothers, our religious superiors who have taught us the truth, our dead and those departed in the faith, especially our relations and those departed who have had a share in the maintenance of this holy place together with those with whom we are in communion, whether by word or deed, in great things or small, and we wish to commemorate in particular N. for whom this sacrifice is offered today.

If the person mentioned is sick, the priest recites three times :

O merciful God, be merciful to N.; grant him a healthy mind and body, through the prayers of your mother and those of your Church.

If the person is deceased, the following is substituted and said three times :

O God who became a sacrifice and to whom sacrifice is offered, be pleased to receive the sacrifice offered with my sinful hands for the soul of N. O God, mercifully grant rest to my father, mother, departed brothers, sisters and relations.

The priest places the vessels upon the altar, the chalice towards the east and the paten towards the west. The whole is then covered with the great veil or annaphuro, while he recites the following :

The heavens are full of the splendour of almighty God, while the earth is filled with the praise of his Name.

The priest descends from the altar, places incense in the censer and recites the following prayers :

Sweet-smelling incense is offered by my weak and sinful hands to the praise and honour of the glorious Trinity. Let us all plead for mercy from the Lord. O God, have mercy on us and assist us.

May we be worthy to offer praise, confession, glory and

prayer, ceaselessly and continuously to the desired fruit which has emerged from the virginal womb and which has made his mother glorious in heaven and on earth.

To this loving Lord, of whom the heavenly choirs sing continuously and who raises the dead by his life-giving spirit, may the praise and honour of this liturgy be given, on this feast-day and at all times forevermore.

The priest takes the thurible and offers incense three times, saying :

O Creator of the world and Architect of the universe, we adore and praise you, O blessed stem that has sprung from a thirsty earth. Mary has given every creature a taste of his wonderful sweetness, and by his glorious doctrine the contagious infection of disbelief has been eradicated.

We offer you, O Lord God, this incense, which we present in imitation of the example set by the priest Aaron, who offered pure incense and kept the plague away from the Israelites.

O Lord God, we beg you to receive this most fragrant incense, which we offer on account of our sins, for the rich and poor, for widows, orphans, the anguished and distressed, for the ill and those who have requested our remembrance, for the living and the dead.

By the supplications of Adam and Eve and those of your mother, Mary, by the prayers of the prophets, apostles, martyrs, confessors, orthodox doctors and by the invocations of the virgins and of all the saints, may we offer you, O Lord, glory, praise and adoration, now and always. Amen.

The priest ascends the altar, and raises the thurible over the Mysteries in the direction of the East, saying :

In this fragrant incense may there be a remembrance of the virgin Mary, mother of God.

Towards the West :

In this fragrant incense, may there be a remembrance of the holy prophets, apostles and martyrs.

Towards the North :

In this fragrant incense, may there be a remembrance of the doctors, priests, the just and holy ones.

Towards the South :

In this fragrant incense may there be a remembrance of the holy Church and all the faithful.

The priest then makes three circles with the thurible over the Mysteries, saying :

> Through your love, O Lord, receive the incense of your servants, and be appeased by the incensing of your priests.
> Be pleased to accept the ministry of those who adore you and may the memory of your mother and your saints be glorified. Be pleased to grant rest to the faithful departed, O Christ our Lord, who is adored and glorified with your Father and the Holy Spirit now and always. Amen.

The priest censes the middle of the altar, saying :

> Adoration to the Father of mercies.

He then censes the north side of the altar, saying :

> Adoration to the compassionate Son.

Then the south side of the altar, saying :

> Adoration to the life-giving Holy Spirit.
> May Mary who bore you and John who baptized you pray for us. Have mercy upon us and may we be considered worthy to offer you the priestly sacrifice, accompanied by the most fragrant of perfumes. May our thoughts, words and deeds be spotless victims and appealing to your divine majesty, and may we always appear before your august presence, through Christ, our Lord. Amen.

The priest descends the steps of the altar and says :

> Kyrie Eleison, Kyrie Eleison, Kyrie Eleison.
> Have mercy upon us, O Lord.
> Enliven us, O Lord, and have mercy upon us.
> O Lord, hear us and have mercy on us.
> Glory to you, O Lord, our eternal hope.
> Pater Noster.

The priest censes the people, and the veil is drawn.

MASS OF THE CATECHUMENS

During the recitation of Psalm 144 (Syriac Bible)—'I will exalt You, O my Lord King'—which is recited in full, a procession is formed around the altar. The priest carries the censer, accompanied by lighted candles borne before him. On returning to the centre of the altar, the priest censes it, the clergy, the people and the Mysteries. (The following text is attributed to Severus of Antioch.)

Choir or priest :   I will exalt you, O my Lord King, the only Son and

Word of the celestial Father, who by your nature are immortal.

Choir :   You were abased and came to give your grace for the living and salvation for the human race.

Choir or Priest :   And were born of the holy, praiseworthy and pure virgin Mary, mother of God.

Choir :   You became man without change and were crucified for us, O Christ our Lord.

Choir or Priest :   Who by your death destroyed our death, by trampling it underfoot. You are one in the holy Trinity.

Choir :   To be adored and glorified with your Father and the Holy Spirit. Have mercy upon us all.

The celebrant takes the Book of the Gospels and is censed by the deacon; the Gospels are placed on a lectern in the sanctuary. The priest ascends the steps of the altar and blesses the mysteries three times and himself three times, then he recites the Trisagion.

Priest :   You are holy, O God.

People :   Have mercy upon us.

Priest :   You are holy, O Strong One.

People :   Have mercy upon us.

Priest :   You are holy, O Immortal One.

People :   Kyrie Eleison, Kyrie Eleison, Kyrie Eleison.

The lessons are normally reduced to two; the 'Apostle', from the Epistles of St Paul, and the Gospel. Each reading is preceded by a secret prayer. The Apostle is read by the deacon from the side door of the screen. Before the Epistle or Praxis, the deacon says the following :

I have heard the blessed Apostle Paul say 'I repeat now the warning we gave you before it happened, if anyone preaches to you what is contrary to the tradition you received, a curse upon him' (*Galatians 1 :9*).

Meanwhile the priest recites the following prayer in silence :

Accept us, O Lord God, and our prayers and requests which are before you at this moment; consider us worthy that with purity and holiness we may keep your commandments, and those of your divine apostles, together with those of Paul, the architect and builder of your holy Church, O our Lord and God forever.

Deacon :   The lesson from the Epistle of the Apostle, Saint Paul to N.

Turning towards the celebrant, he bows his head and says:

> Bless, O Lord!

The priest raises his hand and blesses the deacon, saying:

> Glory to the God of the apostles and may we enjoy his mercies forever.

The deacon now reads the Apostle or Praxis. At its conclusion, the deacon or the people recite the Gradual, which on ordinary days is as follows:

> Alleluia, Alleluia, Alleluia. Offer sacrifice to him, bring gifts and let us go into the presence of God, let us worship him in the Holy of Holies. Alleluia.

Priest in silence: O Lord God, grant us the knowledge of your divine words and imbue us with the understanding of your holy Gospel; be pleased to fill us with the riches of your divine gifts and the presence of your Holy Spirit. May we joyfully observe your commandments and obey them faithfully, and then may we deserve to be considered worthy of your blessings and mercies, now and at all times. Amen.

THE GOSPEL

Deacon: Let us be attentive and respectfully silent. With faith and purity, let us listen to the living words of the Gospel of our Lord Jesus Christ, which is to be presented to us.

People: O Lord, make us worthy to listen to the holy Gospel.

The priest takes the Gospels from the altar and proceeds to the main door of the screen. Facing west, he says:

> Peace be with you all.

People: And with you.

Priest: The holy Gospel of our Lord Jesus Christ, the message of life according to N. the Apostle (*or Evangelist*) which announces the life and salvation of the world.

During the reading of the Gospel which follows, the deacon censes the Gospel and lights are carried. If a bishop is present, he takes off his mitre and lays it on the altar.

Priest: O Lord, save and protect us.

Deacon: He is blessed, who is coming and who will come; may praise be given to him who sent our Saviour and may his mercy be always with us.

Priest: At the time of our Lord God and Saviour Jesus Christ, the life-giving Word, God incarnate from the holy virgin Mary, these things were done . . .

On festivals of our Lady, the following is substituted :

At the time of the feast of the Assumption (*Annunciation, Immaculate Conception, etc.*) of Mary, mother of our Lord God and Saviour Jesus Christ . . .

Deacon and people :   We both believe and confess.

At the conclusion of the Gospel, the priest blesses the congregation with the Book of Gospels and says :

And may peace be with everyone.

The priest bows his head and recites the following prayer secretly.

May our hymns, praises and blessings be given to our Lord Jesus Christ, for his life-giving words to us, to his Father, for having sent his only Son for our salvation, and to the Holy Spirit, the life-giver, now and at all times, forever. Amen.

Deacon :   Let us attend.

People :   O Lord, have mercy upon us.

The Liturgy of the Faithful

The Proem and Sedro that are recited at this point are variable on Sundays and feast-days, and are always recited at the foot of the altar. The Proem and Sedro for ordinary days, is as follows :

May we be considered worthy to offer praise, confession, glory and honour unceasingly and without distraction to Jesus Christ, the great High Priest, the pure and holy Victim, who erased our sins and who in offering himself as a sacrifice brought innocence to a guilty world. To whom belongs praise, honour and power and to his Father and the Holy Spirit, now in this liturgy and on all feasts and moments of our life, forever and ever. Amen.

People :   May it be so.

The priest now puts incense into the censer.

Deacon :   Let us all pray before the merciful God, before his altar of pardon, before these sublime and holy Mysteries and before this terrible Sacrifice, that as incense is poured from the priest's hand, so may we earnestly seek mercy and love from the Lord. O merciful Lord, have mercy upon us and assist us.

THE PRAYER OF PROPITIATION

Priest :   My God, pardon, purify, forget and erase our faults. Through the extent of your mercy, overlook our heinous sins which are innumerable and the sins of all your faithful people. Mercifully look kindly upon us, our fathers, brothers, superiors and our dead and faithful departed, who are sons of the holy and glorious Church. O God, grant rest to their souls and bodies, that they may be refreshed by the affluence of your mercy.

O Christ, our King and our God, hear us and grant us your help and deliverance. In accepting our prayers, be pleased to save us from your cruel punishments and retaliation, O Lord of peace and refuge. Finally may we be granted a most Christian end according to your holy will, and may we always offer you glory and thanksgiving, for ever and ever. Amen.

Deacon :   Amen.

Priest :   O God, Lord of every created thing, who receive the sacrifice of thanksgiving from everyone who calls upon you with heartfelt sincerity, be pleased to accept this incense which is offered to you by the hands of your unworthy servant. Make us worthy to approach your holy altar, and grant that we may be able to offer sacrifices and spiritual offerings for our sins and the sins of your people. Grant that our sacrifice may be acceptable to you and that the Holy Spirit may descend upon us, these gifts and on all your people, who believe in Jesus Christ our Lord.

Deacon :   Amen.

The altar, celebrant, choir and people are then censed, and the altar is censed a second time. The priest, half turned towards the people, says :

May peace be with you all.

Deacon :   And with your spirit. May the Lord receive your prayers and give us every assistance.

Priest :   May God grant us the remission of our faults, the forgiveness of our sins and a holy remembrance for the faithful departed, forever and ever.

Deacon :   Amen.

The priest blesses the censer, after signing himself first. He holds one of the chains in his left hand and says the following prayer while he blesses with his right hand :

Holy is the Father.

Deacon : Amen.

Again the priest blesses himself and takes hold of two chains, while saying :

Holy is the Son.

Deacon : Amen.

The priest blesses himself and then grasps all the chains, while saying :

Holy is the living and Holy Spirit who sanctifies the incense of the sinner, his servant; who is propitious and who has pity upon us, the souls of our relations and friends, our dead and all the faithful departed, who are faithful to the holy Church in both worlds, forever and ever.

Deacon : Amen. Sophia Theo proschomen. Let us stand and recite with attention the prayer of our honoured father, saying, We believe in one God . . .

The priest stands at the foot of the altar. The faithful join the deacon in reciting the creed, while the priest censes the altar three times, the Mysteries, the clergy and the people :

I believe in one God, the Father almighty, maker of heaven and earth, and of all things visible and invisible.

And in one Lord Jesus Christ, the only-begotten Son of God, born of the Father before all ages. God of God, light of light, true God of true God. Begotten not made, being of one substance with the Father, by whom all things were made. Who for us men and for our salvation came down from heaven and was incarnate by the Holy Spirit of the Virgin Mary and was made man. He was crucified also for us, suffered under Pontius Pilate, and was buried. And the third day he rose again according to the Scriptures, and ascended into heaven, and sat at the right hand of the Father. And he shall come again with glory to judge both the living and the dead, of whose kingdom there shall be no end.

And I believe in the Holy Spirit, the Lord and giver of life, who proceeds from the Father and the Son, who together with the Father and the Son is adored and glorified, who has spoken by the prophets.

And in one, holy, catholic and apostolic Church. I confess one baptism for the remission of sins and I look for the resurrection of the dead and the life of the world to come. Amen.

The priest then proceeds to the Lavabo where he washes his fingers while reciting this prayer :

Wash away, O Lord, the evil stains of my soul and cleanse

me with the waters of spiritual life, that I may be deemed worthy to enter the Holy of Holies in purity and holiness; so that without any defilement I may handle your adorable and divine Mysteries and so with a pure conscience offer you a living Sacrifice, that is most pleasing to your Godhead, and like your glorious Sacrifice, Our Lord and Our God, forever and ever. Amen.

The priest turns towards the people, saying :

Pray for me, my brethren and friends.

The priest then bows or kneels in front of the altar and says :

O holy and glorious Trinity, have mercy upon me. O holy and glorious Trinity forgive me my sins. O holy and glorious Trinity receive this offering from my weak and sinful hands. Out of your mercy, O God, be pleased to remember your mother and your saints, and all the faithful departed.

O God, in this hour pardon and remit all the sins of your sinful servant, help me in my human weakness and by the intercession of your mother and all the saints, O God, may you grant pardon and forgiveness to our relations and our superiors and in particular N., for whom this sacrifice is being offered.

THE ANAPHORA OF ST JAMES

The priest ascends the altar and kisses it. The first prayer of the Anaphora the 'Prayer of the Peace', is recited aloud with the hands folded on the breast :

O God, lover of all men, make us worthy of this salvation, and you Who cleansed all from the stain of guilt and hypocrisy, grant that we may be able to salute one another with a holy and divine kiss, and so be united with the bond of love and peace, through our Lord and Saviour Jesus Christ, your only Son, our Lord, through whom and with whom to you belong the glory, honour and dominion with your Spirit, all-holy, good, adorable, life-giving and consubstantial with you, now and forever, worlds unending.

Deacon :   Amen.

Priest :   Peace be to you all.

The method of bestowing the Pax varies. Sometimes the deacon takes the priest's joined hands between his own. These he passes down the length of his own face. The deacon then gives his hands likewise to the next and so on round the church. An alternative method consists in the deacon censing the priest, who catches the smoke in his hands, and puts it to his face ; the deacon then censes the rest of the clergy who do likewise. The next prayer of the Anaphora is called the Prayer of the Inclination and is followed by the Prayer of the Veil, said with folded hands.

People :   And with your spirit.

Deacon :   Let us bow our heads before the Lord.

People :   Before you, O Lord.

Priest :   O merciful Lord, send your blessings upon those who bow their heads before your holy altar. O you who, though so mighty, have regard for the lowly, bless them through the grace, mercies and love that was borne for mankind by Christ, your only Son, through whom and with whom, to you belong glory, honour and dominion with your Spirit, all-holy, good, adorable, life-giving and consubstantial with you, now and ever, worlds unceasing.

People :   Amen.

Priest :   O God, the Father, who out of your great and immeasurable love of mankind sent your Son into the world to bring back the stray sheep, do not turn away from us as we offer this fearful and unbloody Sacrifice, for we have no trust in our own virtue, but only in your mercy. We earnestly beg of your goodness that this Mystery be not for our judgment, but for the eradication of our sins and the punishment due, and for thanksgiving owed to you. Through the grace, mercy and condescension of your only Son, through whom and with whom, to you belong glory, honour and dominion with your Spirit, all-holy, good, adorable, life-giving and consubstantial with you, now and forever, worlds unceasing.

People :   Amen.

The priest removes the veil covering the Elements. He raises and lowers it three times, saying in a low voice :

You are the corner-stone, from which arose the twelve rivers of water which provided for the twelve tribes of Israel. You are the corner-stone which was placed on our Saviour's tomb.

Deacon :   Let us prepare ourselves worthily, with fear, purity, holiness, charity and true faith, but above all with fear; let us look upon this holy Sacrifice which is set before us, and which offers itself for us, a living Victim, to God the Father, by the hands of his priest.

The priest, blessing himself and everyone else, says the following :

The love of God the Father ✠ and the grace of the only begotten Son ✠ the fellowship of the Holy Spirit ✠ and his descent upon you all, my brethren ✠✠✠ forever-more.

People :   And with your spirit.

Priest :   May the hearts and minds of all of us be on high.

At this point, the priest having blessed everybody, turns to the altar and raises his eyes and hands, while the Preface is begun.

People :   They are with the Lord our God.

Priest :   Let us give thanks to the Lord with fear.

People :   It is meet and right.

The Preface consists of two parts. The first is said secretly, while the priest bows down and flutters his right hand over the paten and his left hand over the chalice. The second part of the Preface is recited aloud, and the priest stretches out his hands.

It is very meet, right and fitting and our duty to praise you, to bless you, to celebrate you, to worship you and to give thanks to you, the Creator of every creature, visible and invisible.

In a loud voice : Whom the heavens and the heaven of heavens praise and all their armies, the sun, the moon and the myriads of stars, the earth and the sea with all their inhabitants, the heavenly Jerusalem, the Church of the First-born, that have their names inscribed in heaven, the angels, the arch-angles, the principalities, the powers, thrones, dominations and virtues high above the world, the heavenly servants, the many-eyed cherubim and the six-winged seraphim, who with two of their wings veil their faces and with two other wings cover their feet and with two they fly to one another, unceasingly voicing a hymn of victory, majesty and sublime glory, crying, shouting and saying:
Holy, Holy, Holy.

In Catholic rites, a bell is rung and fans, when available, are shaken. The people respond :

Holy, Holy, Holy.

Fluttering his hands over the Elements, the priest continues :

You are truly holy, King of the worlds and Giver of all holiness. Holy also is your only Son, our Lord and Saviour Jesus Christ; holy also is your Holy Spirit, who searches all things. For holy are you, omnipotent, of fellow feeling for your creatures, who created man out of the earth and gave him the pleasures of paradise. But when man fell, you did not pass him by or forsake him, O God, but you corrected him as an exceedingly merciful Father.

You have called man by the Law, you have instructed him by the Prophets and finally you sent your only Son into the world that he might become incarnate of the Holy Spirit and of Mary, the holy mother of God and ever a Virgin; and he conversed with men and did everything for the redemption of our race.

THE CONSECRATION

Priest, aloud : And when he was about to accept a voluntary death for us sinners, himself being without sin, in the same night in which he was delivered up for the salvation and life of the world, he took bread, *(the priest takes up one bread from the paten, places it in the palm of his left hand, and continues)* in his holy, spotless and unpolluted hands, and showing it to you, God, the Father and when he had given thanks ✠ he blessed ✠ hallowed ✠ broke *(the priest breaks the bread carefully at one of the middle crosses, not separating the halves)* and gave to his disciples and holy apostles saying, Take, eat of it, THIS IS MY BODY, which is given for you and for many is broken *(the priest turns the bread a half circle on the left and breaks it slightly at the bottom, not dividing it completely)* and given for the remission of sins and for eternal life *(the priest lays the bread on the paten)*.

People : Amen.

The sanctuary bell is rung, and if possible, lights are carried and the fans are usually shaken. The Blessed Sacrament is censed and the priest worships.

Priest : And likewise also the cup *(the priest takes the chalice by the middle knop in his right hand and lifts it over the mensa of the altar)* after he had supped, when he had mixed wine and water, he gave thanks ✠ blessed ✠ hallowed ✠ and gave it to his disciples and holy apostles saying, Drink some of it, all of you, THIS IS MY BLOOD *(the priest places his right hand on the lip of the chalice)* of the New Testament, which is shed for you and for many *(the priest then lifts the chalice slightly over the mensa, moves it in a crosswise manner, replaces it and then worships it)* and given for the remission of sins and for eternal life.

People : Amen.

Priest : Do this in memory of me. Every time you eat this bread and drink this cup, you will be proclaiming my death and confessing my resurrection.

People :   We commemorate your death and resurrection, O Lord, and we confess our belief and wait for your second coming. We implore mercy, compassion and forgiveness of our sins. May we receive the fullness of your mercies.

ANAMNESIS

Priest :   Therefore, O Lord, commemorating your death and resurrection on the third day from the tomb and your ascension into heaven and your sitting at the right hand of God the Father, as well as your second coming when you will judge the living and the dead and render to each according as we deserve, we offer you this fearful and unbloody Sacrifice, that you will not deal with us as we really deserve, but rather as your gentleness and regard for men prompt. Erase the sins of us, your suppliants. That is why your people, who are your heritage, implore you and through you and with you, implore your Father, by saying:

People :   Have mercy upon us, O God, the Father almighty, have mercy upon us.

EPICLESIS

During the Epiclesis, the deacon censes the Mysteries. The priest says :

We also give you thanks, while receiving your gifts, O Lord, and we praise you for everything.

The deacon says the following prayer aloud, while the priest recites the Epiclesis :

Let us stand and pray in silence and fear. May the peace and tranquillity of our heavenly Father be with us. Kyrie Eleison, Kyrie Eleison, Kyrie Eleison.

The priest flutters his hands three times over the Mysteries and invokes the Holy Spirit :

Have mercy upon us, O God the Father Almighty and send down your Holy Spirit, the Lord and Giver of life who is equal to you on the throne and equal to the Son in his kingdom, consubstantial and coeternal, who spoke in the Law and the Prophets and through your New Testament, and who came down in the appearance of a dove on our Lord Jesus Christ in the River Jordan and who descended upon the holy Apostles like so many tongues of fire.

People :   Kyrie Eleison, Kyrie Eleison, Kyrie Eleison.

The priest flutters his right hand over the Host three times, blessing it three times. He blesses the chalice similarly. After each part of the Epiclesis, he makes an inclination. At the conclusion, he stands upright and with out-stretched hands completes the Epiclesis :

Priest : That coming down he make this bread the Body ✠ of Christ,
Amen; the life-giving Body, the redeeming Body ✠ of our
souls and bodies, the very Body ✠ of our great Lord God and
Saviour Jesus Christ for the remission of sins and eternal
life to them that receive.

People : Amen.

Priest : And the mixture that is in this cup, the Blood ✠ of Christ,
Amen; the Blood ✠ purifying our souls and bodies, the very
Blood ✠ of our Lord, God and Saviour, Jesus Christ, for
the remission of sins and eternal life to those who receive it.

People : Amen.

Priest, with outstretched arms :

That they may be the Body and Blood of Jesus Christ to all
who receive them and who partake of them. May their souls
and bodies be hallowed and the good works that they do;
may they be fruitful and your Church may it be confirmed,
and grant that the gates of hell will not prevail against it
and that it will be preserved free of heresy, until the end of
the world.

People : Amen.

THE INTERCESSION

The Intercession consists of six parts: three prayers for the living (the faithful brethren, faithful kings and one's father) and three prayers for the dead (mother of God, the fathers and doctors of the Church, and the dead in general). Each prayer consists of two parts : the first part is said secretly by the priest, bowing down with folded hands, while the deacon recites the Diptych aloud, and the people respond at the conclusion by answering either 'Kyrie Eleison' or 'Amen'. The second part is said aloud by the priest with outstretched arms; at its conclusion, the priest lowers his arms and places them over the Mysteries; the people reply 'Amen'. During the recitation of this Intercession the priest blesses the Host with a cross made with the thumb, and then he does likewise on the list of the names of the departed.

Therefore, O Lord, we offer you this fearful and unbloody
Sacrifice, for these your holy places, which you have enhanced by the manifestation of Christ your Son, and
especially for holy Sion, the mother of all Orthodox
Churches, and for your holy Church worldwide. Give her
the rich gifts of your Holy Spirit. And remember, O Lord,
our holy bishops, especially the fathers, our Patriarch Mar
N. and our bishop. Grant them, O Lord, a long life; preserve

them in their task of directing your people in piety and goodness.

Diptych read by the deacon :

O Lord, bless. We pray and beg you, O our Lord and God, at this terrible and holy moment, for all our fathers and rulers who stand in a position of authority over us, and who tend and rule the holy Churches of God in all parts of the world, especially for our holy and revered fathers, the great Pontiff Mar N. Pope of Rome, and Mar Ignatius N. our Patriarch, and our father Mar N. and our sacred Metropolitan N. May they be utterly confirmed in God, with the rest of all the Orthodox bishops. May their prayers be a protection for us; for this let us earnestly beg the Lord.

Priest, silently : For those of our relations and brethren who are in prison or exile, for those who are sick, ill or in any way distressed, O Lord, we beg you to remember, as well as having consideration for the air, the rains, the dews and the fruits of the earth.

Aloud : Deliver us, O Lord, from all oppression and the spite and evil of wicked men, as well as the violent force of the devils. Deliver us as well, O Lord, from all pestilences sent to us by you on account of our sins. Preserve in us the Orthodox Faith and our determination to observe all your life-giving commandments, so that we may be considered worthy to appear before you and to wait for the richness of your mercy to rain upon us. For you, O God, are merciful, and to you we offer glory, as well as to your only Son and the Holy Spirit, all-holy, good, adorable, life-giving and consubstantial with you, now and forevermore.

People : Amen.

Diptych read by the deacon :

Again, we commemorate all our faithful brethren who have asked us to remember them at this time. We also wish to remember all those who have been subject to terrible temptations and who seek their refuge in you. We also pray for this city preserved by God; maintain us in concord and peacefulness, we beg of you, O Lord.

Priest, silently : Again graciously remember those who stand with us and who pray with us, our fathers, brothers, and those who are absent. O Lord, remember those who have asked us to remember them in our prayers; to each one, O Lord, grant the requests that relate to their salvation. Also, O Lord, remember those who have presented their gifts at your altar, those for whom each has offered and especially those who

have wished to offer and could not. Remember those who
are in anyone's mind and those whom we mention by name.

Aloud :   Remember, O Lord, those whom we have mentioned and
those whom we have omitted. According to the magnitude
of your mercy, grant them the joy of your salvation, receiving
their sacrifices and grant them the consolation of your
assistance; strengthen them with your power and might,
because you are merciful and delight in being merciful. To
you therefore belong honour, glory and power with your
only Son and the Holy Spirit.

People :   Amen.

Priest, silently :   O Lord, remember our religious kings and queens,
give them every strength and assistance. Subdue all their
enemies and those that fight against them, so that we may
live a peaceful and quiet life in goodness and humility.

Deacon, aloud :   Again we commemorate all faithful and true Christian
kings who in the world have founded and established
churches and monasteries of God. We also pray for every
Christian government, for the clergy and faithful, that they
may persevere in virtue. For this let us earnestly beg the
Lord.

Priest, aloud :   For you are a refuge and salvation, a helping Power
and victorious Leader of all who call upon your assistance
and have confidence in you. To you belong glory, honour
and power with your only Son and the Holy Spirit.

Priest, silently :   Therefore, O Lord, since you have the power of life
and death and are a God of mercy and love towards mankind,
be pleased to remember all those who have been pleasing to
you since the creation of the world, the holy fathers, fore-
fathers, prophets and apostles, John the Baptist, forerunner
of the Lord, St Stephen, chief of deacons and first of
martyrs, and the holy and glorious mother of God, the ever-
virgin Mary and all the saints.

Deacon, aloud :   Again we commemorate her who is called blessed and
who is glorified by all the generations of the earth, the holy
and blessed, ever-virgin mother of God, Mary. Together
with her let us also remember the prophets, apostles, evangelists, preachers, martyrs and confessors, Blessed John the
Baptist, the holy and glorious Mar Stephen, chief of deacons
and first martyr. Therefore let us remember all the saints.
For this let us earnestly beg the Lord.

Priest, aloud :   Unite us to the blessed Church, give us a place in the
Church by virtue of your grace, and number us among the

first-born whose names are known in heaven. For this reason we remember those who stand before your throne, so that they may have pity upon our misery and poverty, and that they will offer this fearful and unbloody Sacrifice with us, for the assurance of us who are miserable and unworthy, as well as for the repose of all who have fallen asleep in the belief of the truth, our fathers and brethren.

Priest, silently :   Remember also, O Lord, all our holy bishops who have died, and who interpreted the word of truth for us; who from James the archbishop and apostle-martyr even until the present day have preached the Orthodox word of truth to us in this holy Church.

Deacon, aloud :   Again therefore we remember those who have died in holiness having kept the faith undefiled, the apostolic faith which they delivered to us. We also remember the three pious, holy and ecumenic synods of Nicaea, Constantinople and Ephesus, as well as the God-fearing fathers and doctors—James, the brother of our Lord, who was both an apostle and martyr; Archbishop Ignatius, Dionysius, Athanasius, Basil, Gregory, Eustathius and John, but chiefly Cyril, who was a tower of truth and who expounded the Incarnation of the Word of God; and Mar James and Mar Ephraim who were eloquent supports of our holy Church, and all those who have kept the one Orthodox and uncorrupted faith and delivered it to us. Let us beg from the Lord.

Priest, aloud :   May the prayers and supplications of the leading lights and teachers of the Church, who have fought the good fight and who have carried the holy Name before unbelievers, kings and the children of Israel, bring us peace, and may their doctrines be confirmed in our souls. May every heresy which troubles us be speedily destroyed and may we be able to stand before your dread judgment seat, without shame. Because you, O Lord, are holy and dwell in the holy place; to you, the perfector of all saints, we offer glory and thanksgiving.

People :   Amen.

Deacon, aloud :   Again we remember all the faithful departed, particularly those who have departed from this church, town and place; also all those who have departed in the faith and are at rest in your heavenly glory, O God, Lord of spirits and of all flesh. Let us beg Christ our God, who has received their souls and spirits, to grant them, through his great mercy, full pardon and remission of their sins; we entreat him to bring us and them to his heavenly kingdom.

Together let us say three times Kyrie Eleison.

Priest, silently :   O Lord, remember all those Orthodox priests who have died, as well as the deacons, subdeacons, singers, readers, interpreters, exorcists, monks, solitaries, hearers, perpetual virgins and seculars, who have died in the faith, as well as those for whom each has offered the Sacrifice.

Priest, aloud :   O Lord God of spirits and of flesh, remember those whom we have mentioned and those whom we have not mentioned and who have departed from this life in the Orthodox faith. Grant their souls, bodies and spirits eternal rest. Deliver them from the punishment and grant them the consolation of being in Abraham's bosom, where the glory of your divinity is manifested, where all fears and sorrows are banished. Impute not to them their offences; no one is free from defilement except our Lord and Saviour Jesus Christ, your only-begotten Son, through whom we hope to obtain mercies and forgiveness of sins for his sake, both for ourselves and for them.

The people make the following response, while the priest continues silently as below :

People :   Grant them rest; remit and purify the offences and shortcomings of us all, committed knowingly and unwillingly or willingly and unknowingly.

Priest, silently :   Grant them rest, O Lord, and forgive our offences committed by thought, word or deed, whether hidden or manifest, whether known or forgotten and which you alone know.

Priest, aloud :   Preserve us in the faith, and may we be gathered together with your elect, and so be without shame on account of our faults, that in this as in all things your glorious Name will be glorified together with the Name of our Lord Jesus Christ and your Holy Spirit, now and always.

People :   As it has been and always will be, forevermore. Amen.

Priest :   Peace be with you all.

People :   And with you.

The priest places his right hand on the Mysteries, blesses himself and the four corners of the altar; then he turns to bless the people, having blessed the assembled clergy :

May the mercies of the great God and our Saviour Jesus Christ be upon you all, my brethren, forevermore.

THE FRACTION

The priest breaks the bread in the middle, divides and separates the halves; the two halves in his left hand are placed on the paten, which he holds. The priest then takes one piece from the chalice and dips it into the chalice and

signs the left side of the bread with it and then signs the right side similarly.
Then he dips the particle into the chalice again and signs both halves to-
gether. Finally he then places the 'coal' or particle upon the two halves and
replaces the paten upon the altar. During the Fraction, the veil is drawn.

We are breaking the heavenly bread in the Name of the
Father, Amen, ✠ and of the Son, Amen, ✠ and of the living
and Holy Spirit, Amen. ✠ For eternal life. Amen. O Father
of Justice, here is your Son, who sacrifices himself in order
to appease your anger. Accept him because he died for me,
so that I could obtain pardon. Through him, accept this
sacrifice presented by my hands and forgive me.

No longer remember the faults that I have committed
before your majesty. Regard this Blood ✠ shed on Calvary
by evil men. *(A small particle is placed in the chalice, intended*
for the priest's communion.) Hear my prayers because of his
merits. As my faults and offences are so large, so is your
mercy proportionate. But your mercy weighs infinitely
heavier than the greatest mountain.

Regard my sins, but also look upon the sacrifice ✠ offered
for them, the Sacrifice and Victim are infinitely superior to
the sins. It is on account of my sins that your well-loved
Son has undergone such suffering as the piercing with the
nails ✠ and the wound of the lance. His sufferings are
sufficient to appease you and it is by them that I obtain life.
Glory to the Father, who has given us his Son for our
salvation. Adoration to the Son, who has died on the cross
and who has given us life. Honour to the Holy Spirit, who
has begun and accomplished the mystery of our redemption.
O most august Trinity, have mercy upon us.

You are the Christ, our God, whose side was pierced on
Calvary for us. You are the Lamb of God, who takes away
the sins of the world. Forgive our offences and pardon our
sins; grant us the favour of being able to sit at your right
hand. O Lord our God forevermore.

People :   Amen.

THE OUR FATHER

The veil is drawn back and the priest recites the Our Father with out-
stretched arms.

O God, the Father of our Lord Jesus Christ, the Father of
mercies and God of all comfort, who sit above the cherubim
and are glorified by the seraphim, adored by a thousand
times a thousand archangels, tens of thousands of angels,
armies rational and heavenly, you who have sanctified and
perfected the offerings and gifts which are offered as a

fragrant gift, by the grace of your only-begotten Son and by the descent of your Holy Spirit, sanctify our souls and bodies, that with a pure heart and enlightened soul we might shamelessly be so bold as to call upon you, O heavenly Father, almighty and holy, to pray and say: Our Father, who art in heaven . . .

The congregation continues the Pater Noster. The priest adds:

O Lord our God, lead us not into temptation which we are incapable of bearing, but grant us temptations which, being bearable, enable us to be delivered from evil, by Christ our Lord, through whom and with whom to you belong all the glory, honour and dominion with the Spirit, all-holy, good, adorable, life-giving and consubstantial with you, now and forevermore.

People : Amen.

Priest : Peace be with you all.

People : And with you.

Deacon : Let us bow our heads before the Lord.

Priest : Your servants bow their heads down before you, waiting for the richness of your mercies. Send your rich blessings, O Lord, and sanctify our souls, bodies and spirits, that we may be worthy to receive the Body and Blood of the Saviour, by the grace and merciful love of Christ, with whom you are blessed and glorified, both in heaven and on earth, with your Holy Spirit, all-holy, good, adorable, life-giving and consubstantial with you, now and forevermore, without end.

People : Amen.

Priest : Peace be with you all.

People : And with you.

The priest places his hands on the Mysteries, blesses himself and then proceeds to bless those on either side of him and then the congregation :

May the grace and the mercies of the holy, glorious, un-created, essential and eternal, adorable and consubstantial Trinity be with you all forever.

People : Amen.

THE ELEVATION

Deacon : Let us attend and, in fear and trembling, receive your blessing, O Lord.

People : Be propitious, O Lord and have mercy upon us.

The priest places the paten to his eyes, kisses it and then moves it crosswise from East to West and then from North to South, replaces the paten upon the altar and worships. He uncovers the chalice, lifts it and replaces it in a similar manner and worships as before, while the following is said:

> Holy things to holy persons.

People : The one Father is holy, the one Son is holy, the one Spirit is holy.

The same prayers are recited during the elevation of the chalice. During the elevation, the Blessed Sacrament is censed by the deacon, lights are carried and again fans are shaken and the bell is rung.

People : Glory be to the Father, to the Son and to the Holy Spirit, One only forever and ever. Amen.

The priest takes the paten in his right hand and the chalice in his left. He then holds the paten over the chalice, saying:

> The one holy Father is with us, who created the world by his grace.

People : Amen.

Priest : The one holy Son is with us, who has saved us by his own precious sufferings.

People : Amen.

Priest : The one living and Holy Spirit is with us, the Author and Consummator of all things that are and have been. Blessed be the Lord's Name forever more, until the end of the world.

People : Amen.

The priest then places the paten and the chalice on the altar, covering the paten with the star or asterisk and the sacred vessels are then covered with the veils.

THE COMMUNION

The priest recites one of three preparatory prayers while kneeling at the foot of the altar with his hands folded on his breast:

> Grant, O Lord, that I may communicate your Body in holiness and by the consuming of it may my evil desires be driven away, just as by consuming the cup of life, my passions may be slaked, and by you may I be considered worthy of the remission of my faults and the pardon of my sins. O our Lord and our God, forever. Amen.

Or : Grant, O Lord God, that our bodies may be made holy by your holy Body and our souls enlightened by your propitiatory Blood, and may it be for the remission of our faults and the pardon of our sins, O our Lord and our God, forever. Amen.

Or : Grant us, O Lord, to consume your holy Body and to drink your propitiatory Blood and so we may become heirs to your heavenly kingdom, together with all those who have been most pleasing to you, O our Lord and our God, forever. Amen.

During the recitation of one of the above prayers, the deacon recites the following prayer :

Let us remember our fathers who taught us to be children of God in this world. O Son of God, grant them rest in the heavenly kingdom with the just and the righteous in that world which does not pass away.

The priest ascends the altar and, using the spoon, takes the particle out of the chalice ; he says the following prayer, during which the veil is drawn :

I hold you, O God, who controls the world and orders the universe here below. By you may I escape the unquenchable fires and attain the pardoning of my sins, like the sinful woman and the robber. You are our Saviour and our God forever.

The priest lifts the particle in the spoon and continues :

A propitiatory particle of the Body and Blood of Christ our God is given to me, the humble servant and sinner, for the pardon of faults and remission of sins, in both worlds, forever. Amen.

The priest then communicates himself. He then dips the spoon into the chalice and withdraws some of the Sacred Blood, saying :

By your life-giving Blood, shed upon the cross, may my faults be remitted and my sins pardoned, O Jesus, the Word of God, who came to save us. May it be for our resurrection in eternity, our Saviour and our God forever. Amen.

The number of particles necessary for communion are broken off, with care so as to avoid breaking the cross on each particle. These particles are then placed in the chalice and are communicated to the clergy.

Priest : The propitiatory particle of the holy Body and Blood of Christ our God is given to the pious priest *(modest deacon ; faithful subdeacon ; Antonian monk)* and steward of the house of God, for the pardon of offences and the forgiveness of sins. His prayer be with us. Amen.

The veil is opened.

COMMUNION OF THE PEOPLE

The priest takes the covered paten and the chalice, holding the paten in his right and the chalice in his left. He recites the following prayer aloud as he leaves the altar :

> May pardon come down upon these servants, O Son of God, who came for our salvation and shall come for our resurrection and the regeneration of the human race, forever.

People :   Amen.

The priest blesses the people with the paten crosswise, saying :

> O Lord, stretch out your right hand and bless these worshippers who receive your Body and precious Blood for the pardon of their faults and the remission of sins and for the recovery of innocence, before you, O our Lord and our God forever.

People :   Amen.

The priest crosses his right hand over the left, descends the steps to the place for the distribution of communion.

Deacon :   Glory to God in heaven, exaltation to his holy mother, a crown of praise to the martyrs, and pity and mercy for the dead.

The formula for communion is the same as in the communion of the clergy, but the phrase 'pious priest', etc., is replaced by the expression 'true believer'. The communion is given by intinction with either the spoon or by hand. Following the communion of the faithful, the priest blesses the people with the paten, and then similarly with the chalice, saying :

> Glory to you, glory to you, our Lord God forever, O our Lord Jesus Christ. Do not permit the Body which we have eaten and the Blood which we have drunk be to our judgment and condemnation, but rather be for eternal life and our salvation; be merciful to us.

The priest returns the sacrament to the altar.

Deacon :   Let us pay attention to what we have received.

The priest stands with hands folded on his breast and recites the following prayer aloud :

> We give thanks to you, O Lord God, and in particular we praise you on account of your immense and ineffable love towards mankind, for you have considered us worthy to receive and partake of your holy banquet. Do not condemn us because of our reception of your holy and unspotted Mysteries, but maintain us in justice and holiness, that being

considered worthy to partake of your goodness, we may find our place and inheritance with all the saints who have pleased you in the world, by the grace, mercies and love of mankind that your only Son has, through whom and with whom, belong all the glory and honour and power with the Holy Spirit, now and always forever.

People : Amen.

Priest : Peace be with you all.

People : And with you.

Deacon : Let us bow down our heads before the Lord.

People : Before you, O Lord.

Priest : O God, you who being great and marvellous knows the heavens and came down to earth for the salvation of humanity, have regard for us according to your mercies and grace. Bless your people and preserve us, so that we may always praise you, because you are our true God, with God the Father and the Holy Spirit, now and forever.

People : Amen. Bless us, O Lord.

Deacon : Depart in peace in the name of Christ.

People : In the name of the Lord our God.

The priest usually says a variable prayer at this juncture. The people respond :

By the prayer of your mother and of all your saints, pardon us, O our Lord, and grant rest to our departed. Bless us, O Lord.

The priest half turns towards the people and raises his arms during the blessing :

✠ Go in peace, O our brethren; we commit you to the grace and the mercy of the holy Trinity, with the Viaticum and the blessings which you have received from the purifying altar of the Lord, those close by and those who are absent, the living and the dead, those saved ✠ by the victorious Cross of the Lord and signed by the mark of holy baptism.

May the holy Trinity pardon your sins and forgive your faults; may he give rest to the souls of your dead and have mercy *(bows towards the altar)* on me a miserable sinner and may your prayers help me. ✠ Go in peace while rejoicing and content, and pray for me.

THE ABLUTIONS

The priest descends from the altar and says the following two prayers silently, while the veil is drawn :

By the Sacrifice which we have offered today, may the Lord

God be satisfied, and may remembrance be made of his mother and all the saints and for all the faithful departed and especially him *(her)* for whom and on behalf of whom this Sacrifice has been made today.

Your sacred and holy mouth, O Lord, has promised and said: Whoever eats my Body and drinks my Blood and believes in me and dwells in me and I in him, I will raise him up on the last day. And to us, O Lord, who have eaten your holy Body and drunk your propitiatory Blood, do not allow it to be a judgment against me, for vengeance, condemnation or accusation, nor also for your faithful people, but let it be for the pardon of offences and for the remission of sins and for a blessed resurrection from the dead and for boldness before your judgment seat, O our Lord and our God forever.

The priest ascends the altar, uncovers the chalice and paten, puts the spoon into the chalice and communicates himself with any remaining particles, during which he recites Psalm 23. After cleansing the paten with two fingers, he places it upon the altar and proceeds to consume the contents of the chalice, saying the following prayer, before the ministration:

What reward will I give to the Lord, for all that he has done for me. I will take the chalice of the Lord and call upon the Name of the Lord.

The paten is then washed with wine which is poured into the chalice, and it is consumed by the priest who says:

'They will be satisfied with the generosity of your house . . .' (*and the rest of Psalm 35*).

Water is then put in the paten, the spoon and asterisk are also cleansed and poured into the chalice, and the contents are again consumed. His fingers are then washed in the paten, first his right hand and then his left, accompanied by the recitation of the prayers that appear below. The water is then poured into the chalice and drunk, sometimes by the deacon.

Priest, while cleansing his right hand:

Allow my fingers to practise your praises and my mouth to announce your thanksgiving. By the nails in your feet and hands and by the spear which pierced your side, pardon my offences and my sins.

While cleansing his left hand:

Preserve me from dishonest men and may your right hand assist me; preserve me from wickednesses, forever.

The paten and chalice are now wiped with the sponge, and the priest recites the following prayer:

With the cleansing power of your mercies, erase all my offences and sins committed before your loving pardon, O Christ our King, who have given life and whose Mysteries I have ministered. Count me with the just who have loved you and with the righteous who have wanted to serve you, O my Lord, in your heavenly kingdom, which is never-ending. O my Lord, so be it, now and always.

The priest now arranges the vessels on the diakonikon where he washes his hands again and recites Psalm 24; during the wiping of his hands, Psalm 29 is recited. The priest then takes off his vestments and says a Teshmeshto of the Departed; he then turns towards the altar, kisses it in the middle and then on either side and says the following prayers:

Remain in peace, O holy and divine altar of the Lord. From now on, I do not know whether I shall return to you or not. May the Lord grant me to see you in the Church of the first-born, which is in heaven, and in this covenant I trust.

Remain in peace, O holy and propitiatory altar of the holy Body and Blood, which I have received from you. May it enable me to obtain pardon of my offences and the remission of my sins and boldness before your fearful judgment seat, O our Lord and our God, forever.

Remain in peace, O holy altar and table of life, and beg our Lord Jesus Christ for me, that I may not be forgotten from now until the end of time, through the bountiful mercy of our Lord.

During Lent and on fasts and vigils, bread, called the Blessing or Burk'tho, is blessed and distributed. When there is a sermon, it is after the Gospel among the Syrians; among the Jacobites, it is after the Blessing and before the Fraction, or after the Elevation and before the priest's communion.